MENSA
ALL-COLOR
PUZZLE
BOOK
1

A FIREFLY BOOK

Published by Firefly Books Ltd., 2000

First Printing

Library of Congress Cataloging-in-Publication Data is available.

Canadian Cataloguing in Publication Data

Allen, Robert (Robert P.)
 Mensa all-color puzzle book 1

ISBN 1-55209-498-7

1. Puzzles. I. Skitt, Carolyn. II. Title.

GV1493.A44 2000   793.73   C00-930465-7

First published in the United States in 2000 by
Firefly Books (U.S.) Inc.
P.O. Box 1338, Ellicott Station
Buffalo, New York 14205

First published in Canada in 2000 by
Firefly Books Ltd.
3680 Victoria Park Avenue
Willowdate, Ontario M2H 3K1

Editor: Tim Dedopulos
Design: Paul Messam
Production: Bob Bhamra

Printed in Spain

MENSA ALL-COLOR PUZZLE BOOK 1

Robert Allen

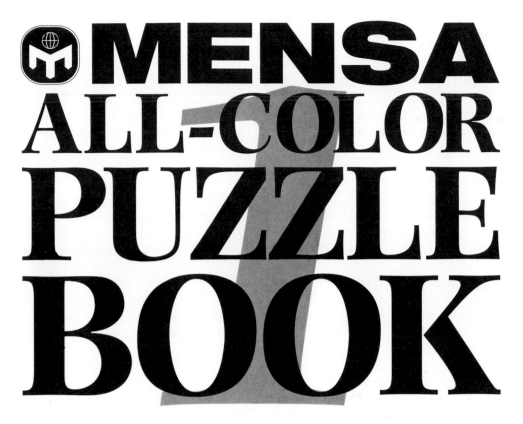

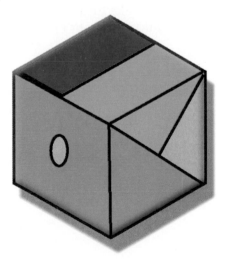

FIREFLY BOOKS

Joining a Mensa society

Mensa Canada and American Mensa are two national branches of the international Mensa society, which includes more than 100,000 people in 80 countries. Members of Mensa have one thing in common: an IQ in the top two percent. Nearly 3,000 Canadians and 45,000 Americans have found out how bright they are and joined Mensa. That leaves millions of people in North America alone who are not Mensa members. You may be one of them.

Looking for mental stimulation?

If you enjoy mental exercise, you'll find lots of good "workout programs" in the magazines published by Mensa Canada and American Mensa. Voice your opinion in one of the newsletters published by local chapters. Learn from the many books and publications that are available to you as a member. Challenge each other at meetings, social events and national gatherings.

Looking for social interaction?

Mensans come from all walks of life, with personalities just as varied. Whatever your interests you will find people with whom you can feel comfortable. Local meetings, parties, get-togethers, lectures, debates, outings and more provide opportunities to exchange ideas and forge new friendships.

Looking for others who share your special interest?

Many Mensa societies include SIGs — special interest groups in which members can enjoy the company of like-minded people, whether your interest is as common as crossword puzzles, as esoteric as Egyptology or as off-the-wall as Monty Python. Some societies have as many as 250 SIGs.

Mensa is about intelligence not education. Take the challenge and discover how smart you really are. You might be surprised. For information or to join, contact your national Mensa society below.

Mensa Canada
329 March Road
Box 11
Kanata, Ontario K2K 2E1
Telephone (613) 599-5897
Fax (613) 599-5897
Email<mensa@igs.net>
WWW<http://www.canada.mensa.org>

American Mensa
1229 Corporate Drive West
Arlington, Texas 76006-6103
Telephone (817) 607-0060
Toll-Free Telephone 1-800-66MENSA
Fax (817) 649-5232
WWW<http://www.us.mensa.org>

Contents

Introduction 6

Introduction

The folks at Mensa are always on the lookout for a way to make life just that bit more difficult for you. Don't get the wrong idea, there is definitely no malice involved here, just a persistent desire to make their puzzles as challenging as humanly possible. Recently there was a sudden flash of inspiration and a voice from above called out, "Why not add color?" Color? Surely that will only make the book look prettier? Then the penny dropped (even Very Intelligent People can be a bit thick sometimes), and they realized that color could be used as an integral part of a puzzle. What an idea! With a little bit of ingenuity color can represent letters or numbers in a whole range of intriguing and entertainingly mystifying ways. A whole new vista of puzzling pleasure opened before their eyes.

Take, for example, the Three Triangles puzzle in which numbers are placed at the points of the triangles and the reader has to work out what they signify and then supply the one number that has been left out. It's an old faithful that, even in its simplest form, is capable of endless complication. Now, suppose you color the sides of the triangle? Then you add colored panels inside, and the colors all represent numbers that bear a simple relationship to each other. In a trice the puzzle is transformed to a cunning conundrum that will take hours of nail-biting pleasure to unravel. Oh yes, when it comes to really making your brain ache, you can depend on Mensa!

Easy Puzzles

PUZZLE 1

Which of these groups of triangles is the odd one out?

Answer see page **80**

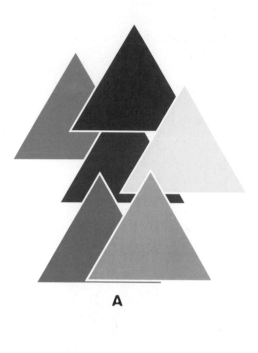

A

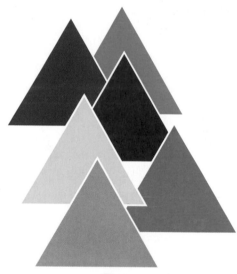

B

C

D

E

PUZZLE 2

These colors should remind you of a certain cocktail.

Answer see page **80**

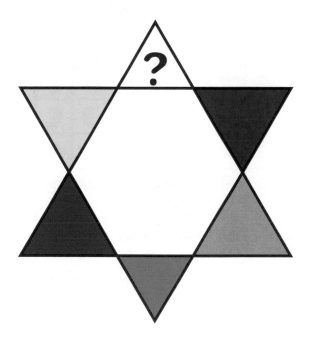

PUZZLE 3

Which triangle should replace the question mark?

Answer see page **80**

PUZZLE 4

The symbols in the above grid follow a
pattern. Can you find the missing section?

Answer see page **80**

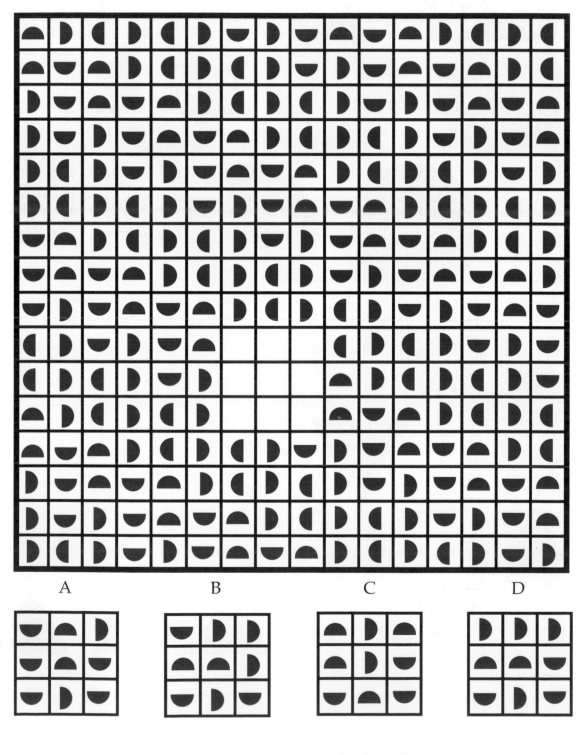

A   B   C   D

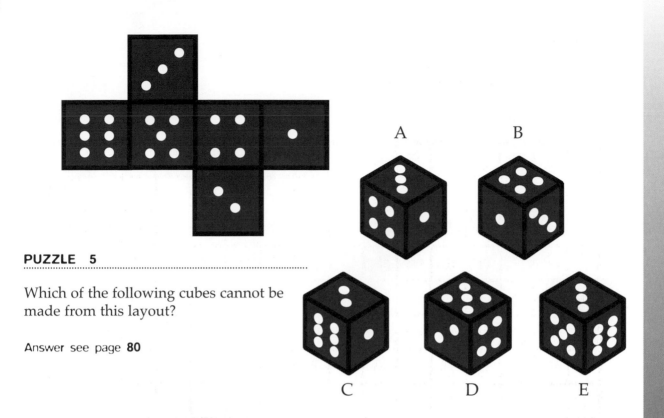

PUZZLE 5

Which of the following cubes cannot be made from this layout?

Answer see page **80**

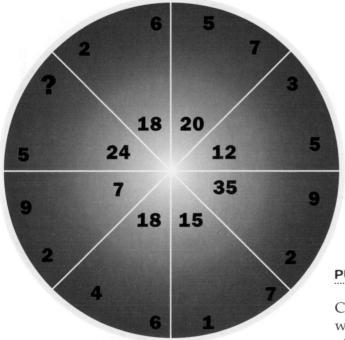

PUZZLE 6

Can you replace the question mark with a number to meet the conditions of the wheel?

Answer see page **80**

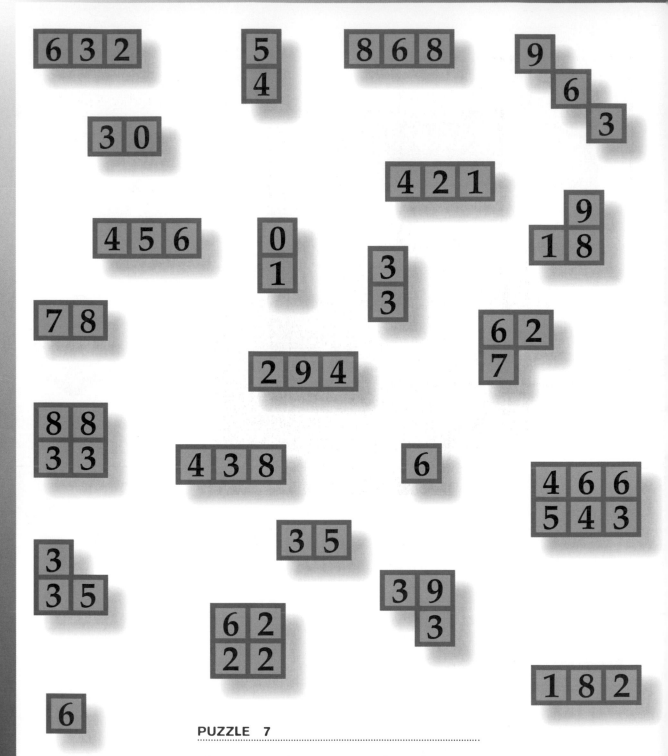

PUZZLE 7

These tiles, when placed in the right order, will form a square in which each horizontal line is identical with one vertical line. Can you successfully form the square?

Answer see page **80**

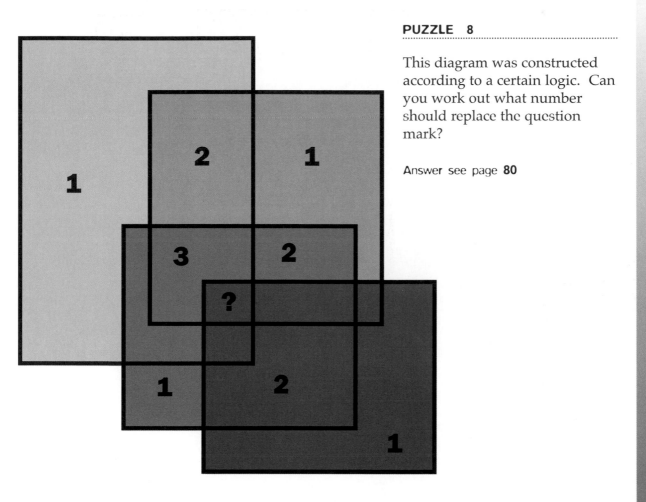

PUZZLE 8

This diagram was constructed according to a certain logic. Can you work out what number should replace the question mark?

Answer see page **80**

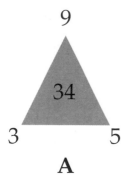
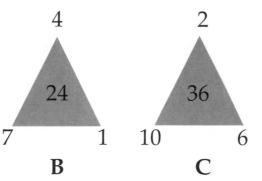
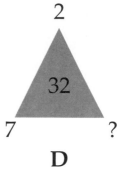

9
34
3   5
A

4
24
7   1
B

2
36
10   6
C

2
32
7   ?
D

PUZZLE 9

Can you find the number to go at the bottom of triangle D?

Answer see page **80**

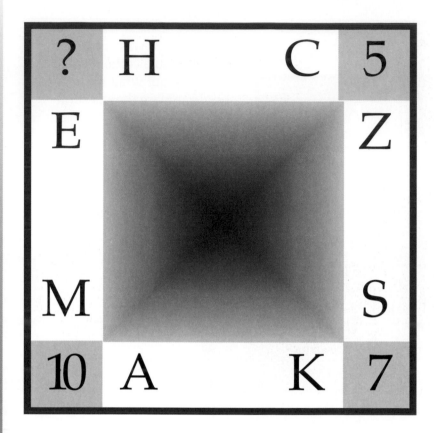

PUZZLE 10

Can you find out the relationship of the letters and numbers in this square and find out what number should replace the question mark?

Answer see page **80**

 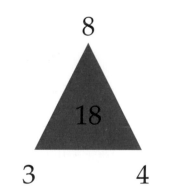 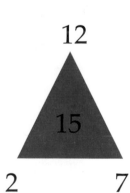 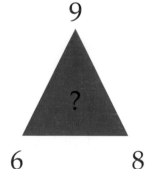

PUZZLE 11

Can you work out how the numbers in the triangles are related and find the missing number?

Answer see page **80**

PUZZLE 12

Can you find the odd ball out?

Answer see page **80**

1

2

PUZZLE 13

Can you work out the time on the blank clock face?

Answer see page **80**

3

4

15

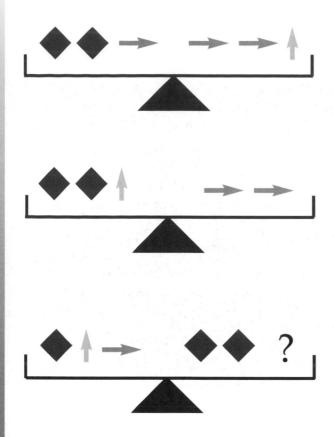

PUZZLE 14

Can you find the symbol that will balance the last set of scales?

Answer see page **80**

PUZZLE 15

The diagram represents an old-fashioned telephone dial with letters as well as numbers. Below is a list of numbers representing ten American states. Can you use the diagram to decode them?

Answer see page **80**

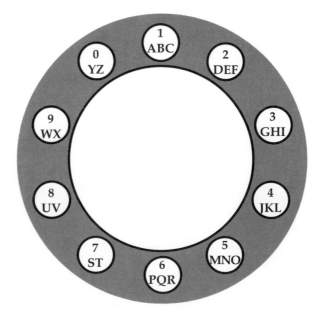

A. 1143256531	**F.** 562355	
B. 72917	**G.** 83633531	
C. 52161741	**H.** 2456321	
D. 141741	**I.** 15456125	
E. 32135	**J.** 1630551	

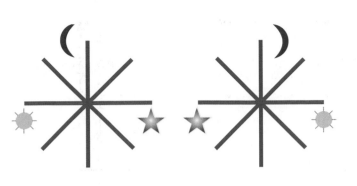

A   is to   B   as   C   is to

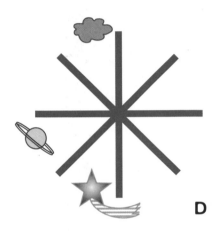

D

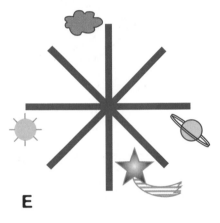

E

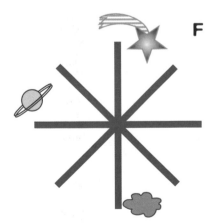

F

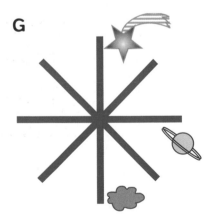

G

PUZZLE 16

Answer see page **80**

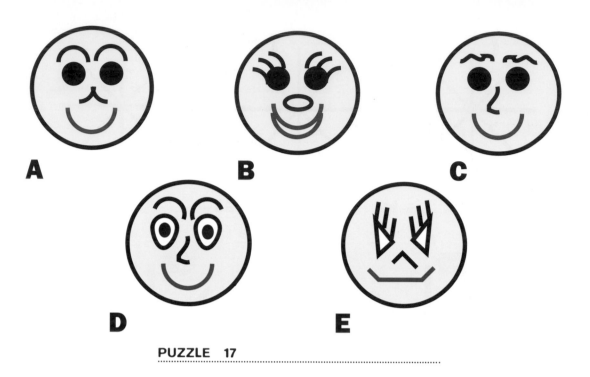

PUZZLE 17

Can you find the odd face out?

Answer see page **80**

PUZZLE 18

Which matchstick man, G, H or I, would carry on the sequence?

Answer see page **80**

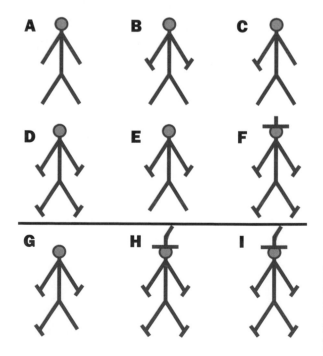

PUZZLE 19

The above clocks move in a certain pattern. Can you work out the time on the last clock?

Answer see page **81**

PUZZLE 20

The letters and numbers in this square follow a pattern. Can you work out what number is represented by the question mark?

Answer see page **81**

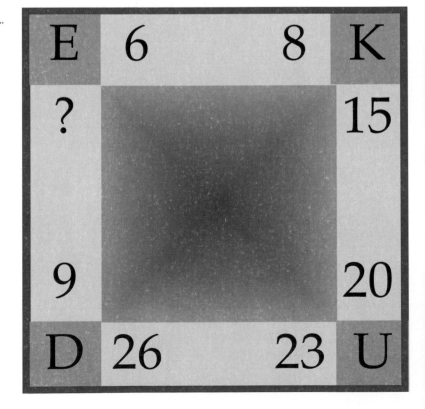

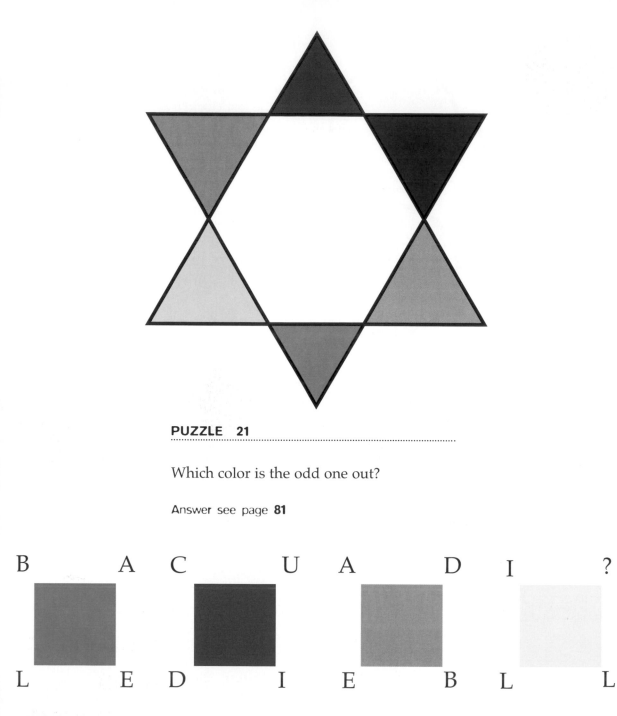

PUZZLE 21

Which color is the odd one out?

Answer see page **81**

B   A   C   U   A   D   I   ?

L   E   D   I   E   B   L   L

PUZZLE 22

Unravel the logic behind these squares to
find the missing letter.

Answer see page **81**

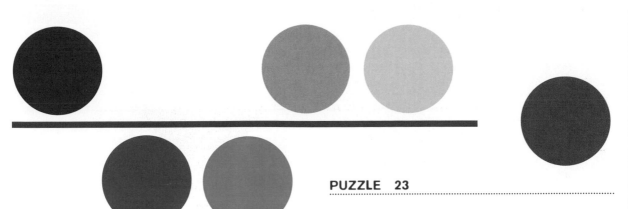

PUZZLE 23

Should Brown go below or above the line?

Answer see page **81**

PUZZLE 24

Does Pink belong with the other colors?

Answer see page **81**

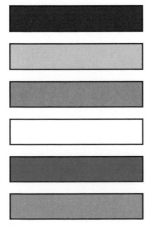

PUZZLE 25

Match the colors with the words.

Answer see page **81**

MOON

CHAMPAGNE

GOLD

SUBMARINE

RAIN

CITY

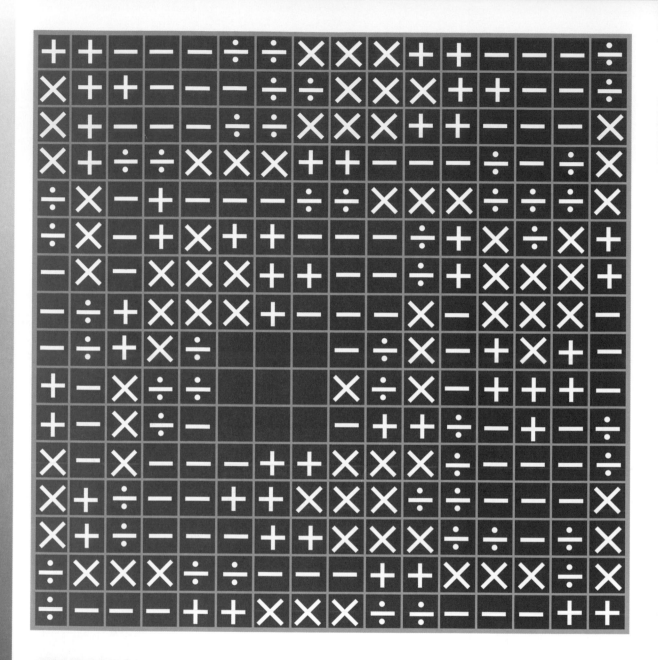

PUZZLE 26

The symbols in the above grid follow a pattern. Can you work it out and find the missing section so that the logic of the grid is restored?

Answer see page **81**

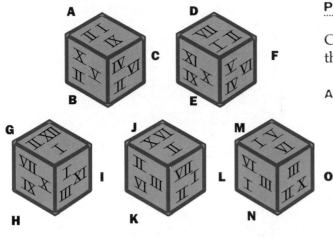

PUZZLE 27

Can you work out which two sides on these cubes contain the same numbers?

Answer see page **81**

PUZZLE 28

Can you find the number to complete the diagram?

Answer see page **81**

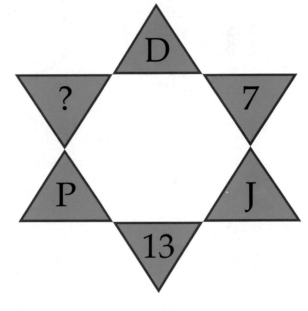

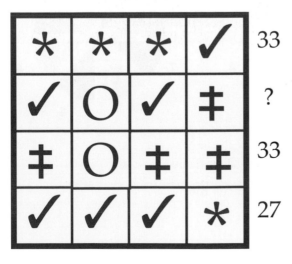

PUZZLE 29

Each symbol in this square represents a value. Can you work out how much the question mark is worth?

Answer see page **81**

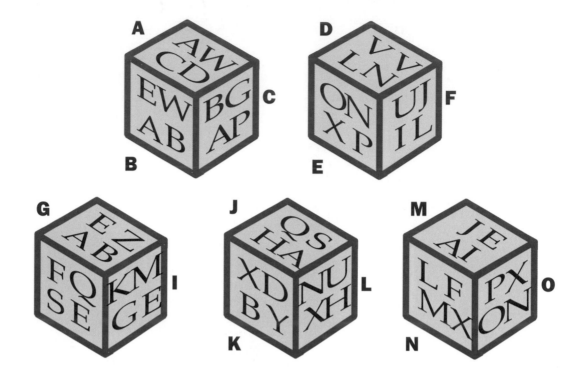

PUZZLE 30

Two sides of these cubes contain the same letters. Can you spot them?

Answer see page **81**

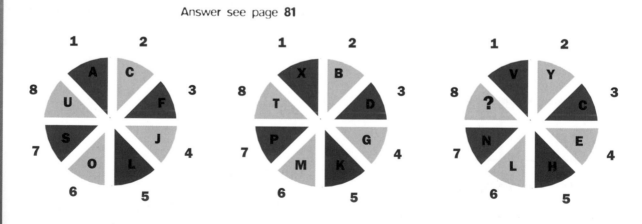

PUZZLE 31

Can you find the letter that replaces the question mark?

Answer see page **81**

```
C W C O A L M K W O E A C K L G O Z A N
L H E M I N G W A Y N E I Y L M O X A E
L E E C M O X K W A X F E X A N B K O S
C F A K K E N Z A E X L A E B L P E F B
A Y E L H M Z N O E X I A I F H R K L I
M O Q V T O A T E U I W E H T E O G M O
A T K V L A V C H A E M N O L E U A B C
F S I A T A M Q L S D I C K E N S S T A
A L S T V E M W M N O E I A C H T A C T
F O O X W A B E A L L E I T A W W A C G
G T O X A E A K F A K I L A A S T A W N
O N F B C H J K W L L T J I I E X G H I
E N O L F M G O Z X A Y N A E B E C W L
R V O L F I G A E Z I U I E J C C K T P
E W U V E C U O P T E G B P N H T S E I
C S E W X H L H J A L E C E K L T U Z K
U A T A E E C K U W P Q R A R A E P A Z
A U S T E N X A T A Q W A L E T A W V E
H A P E X E A B C B A C A E W W E X L E
C C W A O R W E L L K M N O P P E L T U
```

Austen	Hemingway	Michener
Chaucer	Huxley	Orwell
Chekhov	Ibsen	Proust
Dickens	Kafka	Tolstoy
Flaubert	Kipling	Twain
Goethe	Lawrence	Zola

PUZZLE 32

In this grid are hidden the names of 18 famous authors. Can you detect them? You can go forward or in reverse, in horizontal, vertical and diagonal lines.

Answer see page 81

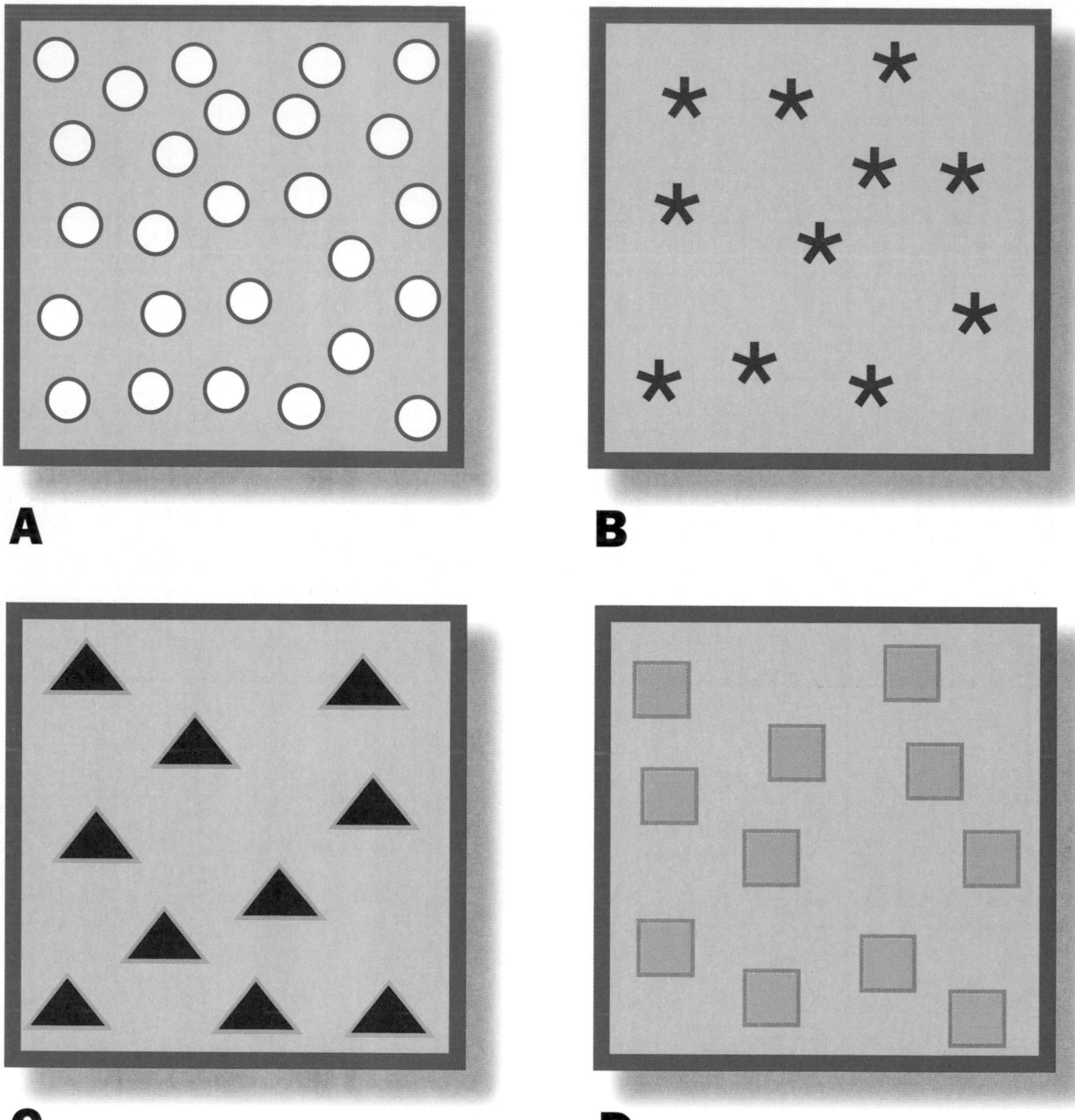

A

B

C

D

PUZZLE 33

There is a logic to the patterns in these squares but one does not fit. Can you find the odd one out?

Answer see page **81**

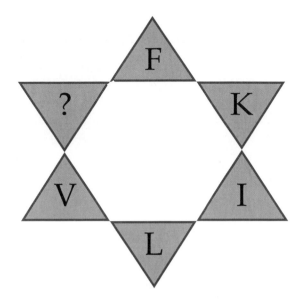

PUZZLE 34

What letter replaces the question mark in this star?

Answer see page **82**

PUZZLE 35

These tiles, when placed in right order, will form a square in which each horizontal line is identical with one vertical line. Can you successfully form the square?

Answer see page **82**

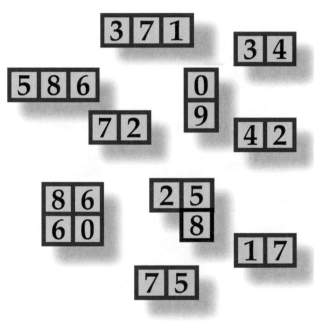

PUZZLE 36

Can you work out what the time on the blank clock face should be?

Answer see page **82**

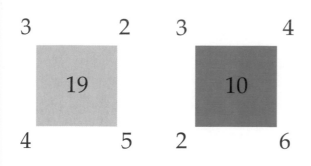 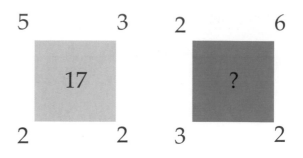

3   2   3   4   5   3   2   6

19   10   17   ?

4   5   2   6   2   2   3   2

PUZZLE 37

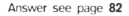

Find the missing number.

Answer see page **82**

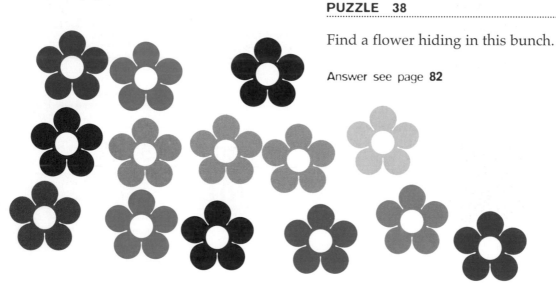

PUZZLE 38

Find a flower hiding in this bunch.

Answer see page **82**

PUZZLE 39

What color of the spectrum could continue this series?

Answer see page **82**

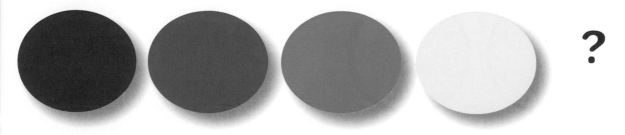

PUZZLE 40

Which of these is the odd one out?

Answer see page **82**

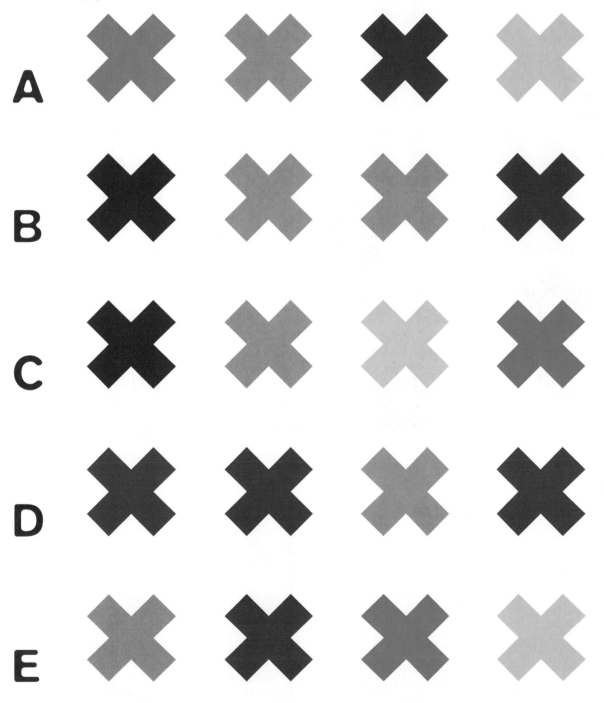

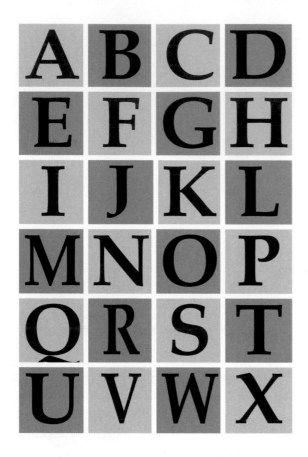

PUZZLE 41

This simple grid turns letters into code numbers. The encoded words are all names of famous painters. Can you decrypt them?

Answer see page **82**

41 34 12 14 52 52 42

53 24 44 13 53 14 43 11 51

22 14 64 22 34 43

31 24 42 43 14 53 11 42

12 42 43 52 51 14 13 31 24

53 14 41 21 14 24 31

63 14 43 22 42 22 21

44 14 51 34 52 52 24

PUZZLE 42

Each symbol in the square on the right represents a number. Can you find out how much the question mark is worth?

Answer see page **82**

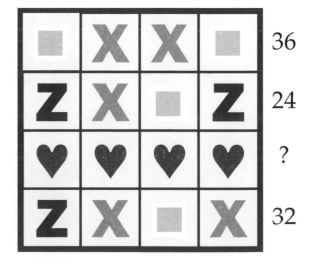

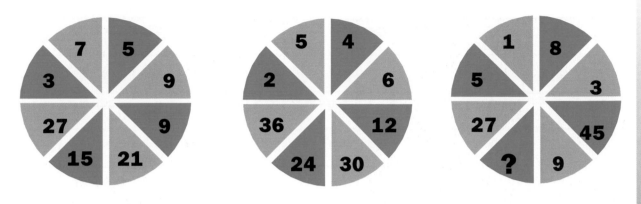

PUZZLE 43

Can you find the missing number that fits into the sector of the last wheel?

Answer see page **82**

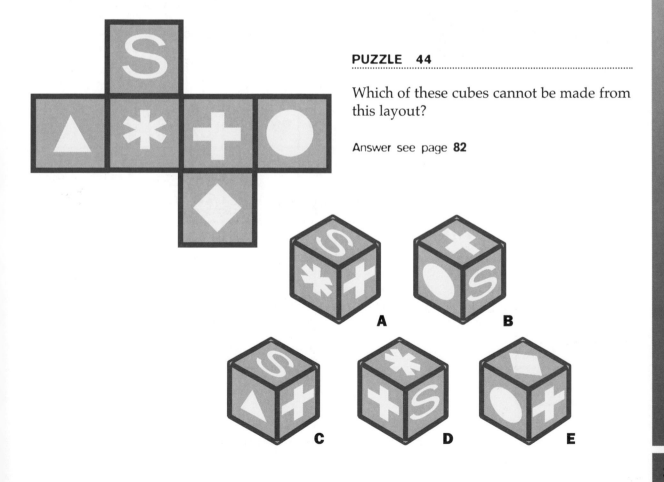

PUZZLE 44

Which of these cubes cannot be made from this layout?

Answer see page **82**

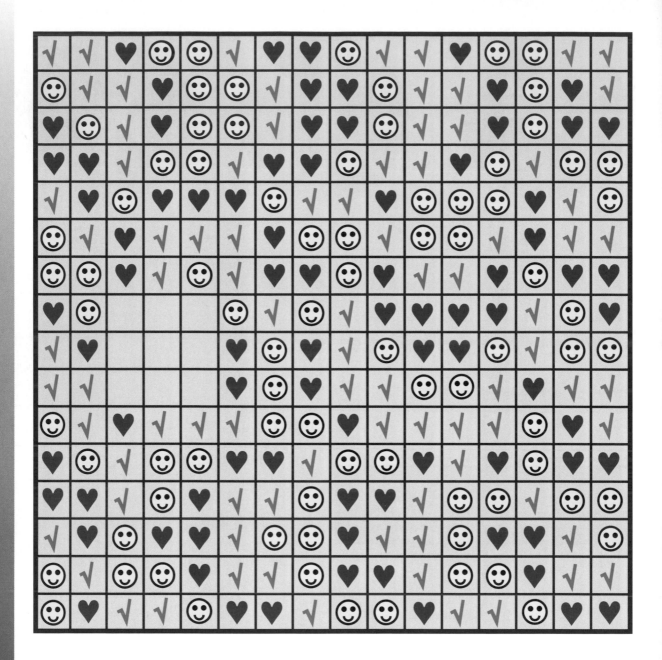

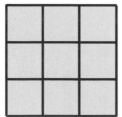

PUZZLE 45

The symbols in the above grid follow a pattern. Can you work it out and find the missing section?

Answer see page **82**

MENSA MENSA MENSA MENSA MENSA MENSA MENSA MENSA

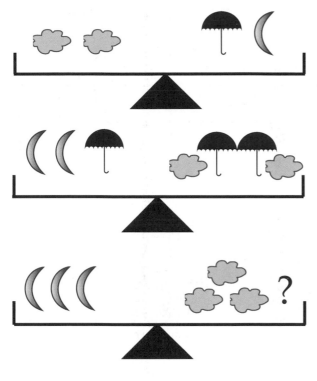

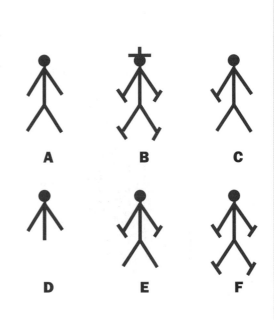

PUZZLE 46

The first two sets of scales are in balance. Which symbol is needed to balance the third set?

Answer see page **82**

PUZZLE 47

Can you spot the odd figure out?

Answer see page **83**

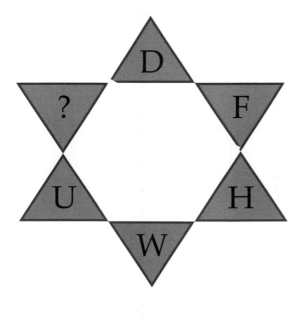

PUZZLE 48

Can you find the letter that completes the star?

Answer see page **83**

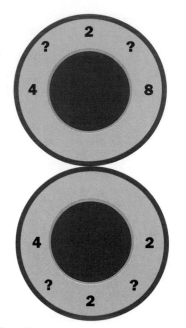

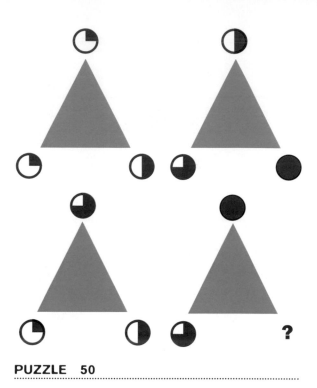

PUZZLE 49

Can you work out what mathematical signs should replace the question marks so that both sections of the diagram arrive at the same value greater than 1. You have a choice between ÷ or x.

Answer see page **83**

PUZZLE 50

Can you find the missing symbol in the last triangle?

Answer see page **83**

36   40   50   23

*	✓	‡	0	38
✓	✓	✓	0	41
*	*	✓	0	?
*	*	‡	*	37

PUZZLE 51

Each symbol in this square represents a value. Can you find out what number should replace the question mark?

Answer see page **83**

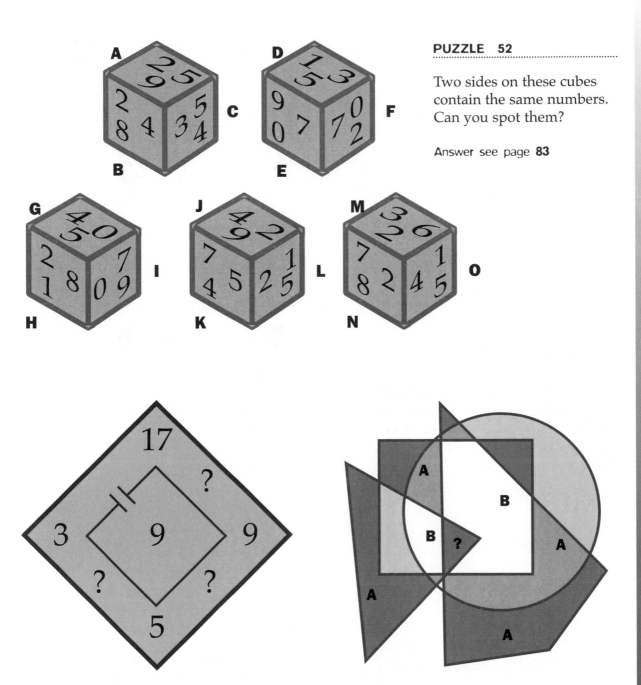

PUZZLE 52

Two sides on these cubes contain the same numbers. Can you spot them?

Answer see page **83**

PUZZLE 53

The mathematical signs in this diamond have been left out. Reading clockwise from the top can you work out what the question marks stand for?

Answer see page **83**

PUZZLE 54

A certain logic has been used in making this diagram. Can you work out what the secret is and replace the question mark with a letter?

Answer see page **83**

```
P B A W N W O C H K T V E N T A C Y X O
A A D E F W O Y J U L I A R O B E R T S
C D U S T I N H O F F M A N B R M O N L
K A O L W O L N N Y G O R E S O T U V D
K M G E N E W I L D E R W O L O Z B R R
C A S K L E M U O T L B W J L K K E G O
P C M W V U W E A I J L G A H E T E B F
E L K E F O Z M A A T H E N A S E R O D
E S O A L L A M A A O I E E O H I L L E
R T A S E G F A A N T O E F L I S T R R
T O M C R U I S E S R S E O T E E E P T
S A O E E B W B I M Q I A N E L G N O R
L A A O H E H R S T D A B D C D O A T E
Y A F G S V H T E O I B K A R S C E J B
R B P O A C F A J Z N A Y A A Y I X Q O
E N O Z E A L M A O C Y H F O G H E L R
M A E I N A Z E N I A C L E A H C I M B
C P L M A N N V W X I E R S F L A Z O N
N U W M J F G Q S R A E L L A E S S O E
J O N Y F G I N O S P M O H T A M M E F
```

Jane Asher

Julia Roberts

Mel Gibson

Julie Christie

Meryl Streep

Paul Newman

Jane Fonda

Gene Wilder

Richard Gere

Michael Caine

Brooke Shields

Dustin Hoffman

Tom Cruise

Emma Thompson

Robert Redford

Jodie Foster

PUZZLE 55

Hidden in this grid are the names of 16 well-known actors. Can you spot them? You can move in horizontal, vertical and diagonal lines in a forward or backward direction.

Answer see page **83**

PUZZLE 56

Which of the faces A, B or C would carry
on the sequence above?

Answer see page **83**

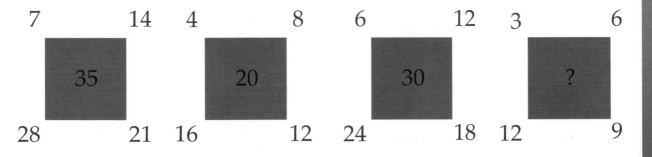

PUZZLE 57

Can you work out what number should
go into the last square?

Answer see page **83**

PUZZLE 58

These tiles when placed in right order will form a square in which each horizontal line is identical with one vertical line. Can you successfully form the square?

Answer see page **83**

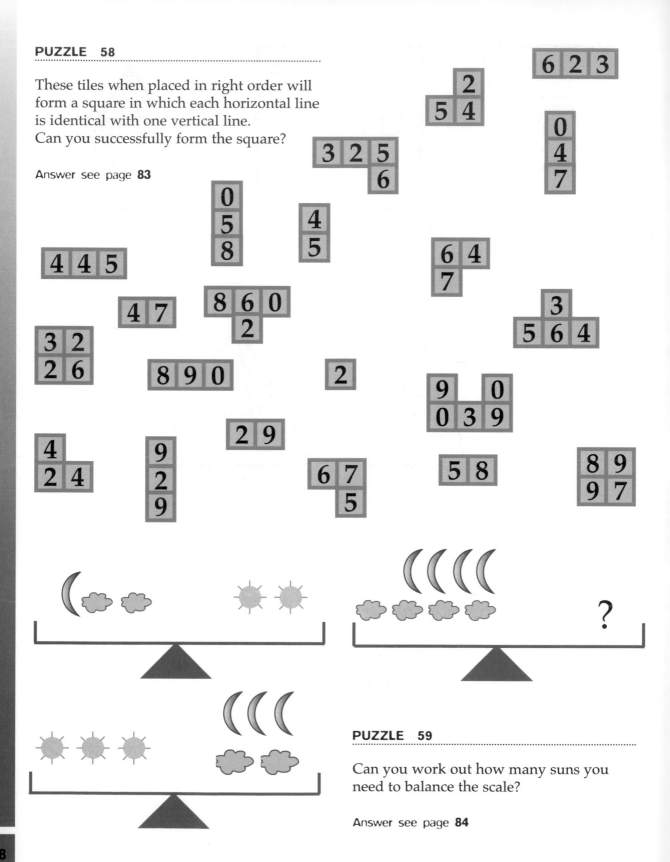

PUZZLE 59

Can you work out how many suns you need to balance the scale?

Answer see page **84**

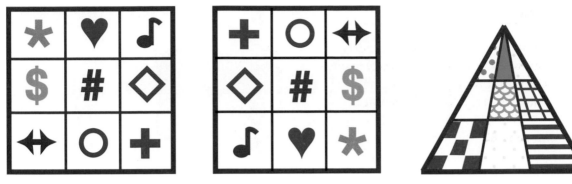

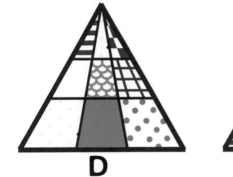 

A is to B as C is to

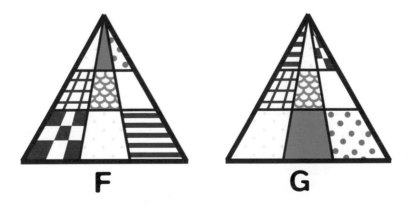

PUZZLE 60

Answer see page **84**

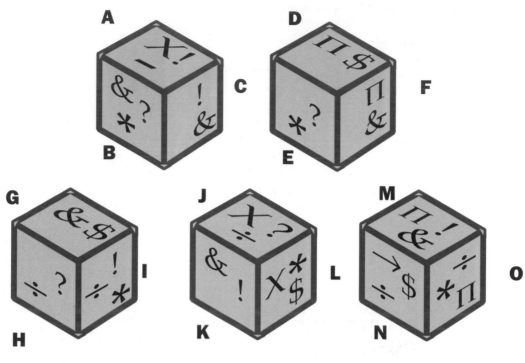

PUZZLE 61

Can you find the two sides on these cubes
that contain the same symbols?

Answer see page **84**

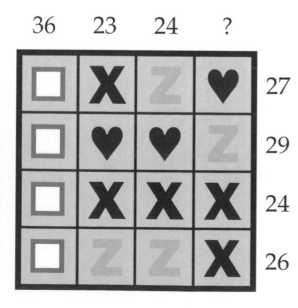

PUZZLE 62

Each symbol in the grid has a numerical
value. Work out what those values
are and replace the question mark with a
number.

Answer see page **84**

K	L	N	B	C	E	W	O	P	Q	B	A	I	K	M	O	L	C
G	A	E	C	C	W	V	R	A	E	I	X	C	M	O	L	A	D
B	E	F	H	A	E	L	E	H	A	R	U	O	H	N	K	M	X
O	A	B	A	C	H	A	N	A	E	X	T	A	T	O	T	E	W
R	L	O	N	E	F	A	G	E	T	W	Y	A	E	X	P	M	M
O	N	A	D	E	A	G	A	H	A	D	H	E	L	L	E	I	E
D	A	C	E	F	G	E	W	A	N	E	A	E	I	M	C	O	N
I	U	F	L	I	S	Z	T	B	E	N	T	V	O	W	L	C	D
N	A	E	K	M	O	Z	G	A	V	E	A	Z	C	K	L	P	E
Q	S	K	A	E	K	E	B	E	O	H	A	R	T	U	E	K	L
L	W	A	A	E	I	P	Q	R	H	R	A	E	T	X	C	K	S
A	C	E	I	R	V	O	S	P	T	Q	V	R	W	B	R	C	S
S	D	A	G	E	O	K	W	O	E	L	X	I	M	N	U	T	O
M	O	V	X	Z	K	V	M	N	E	K	E	C	V	A	P	J	H
H	L	W	X	Q	W	A	D	E	B	U	S	S	Y	A	T	O	N
A	O	W	P	X	B	E	I	E	P	Q	O	Z	A	C	L	T	W
R	A	C	A	S	C	H	U	B	E	R	T	T	O	R	H	D	A
B	B	C	F	K	L	M	N	T	A	C	T	O	A	R	Z	W	I

PUZZLE 63

Bach	Dvorak	Mendelssohn
Beethoven	Grieg	Mozart
Borodin	Handel	Purcell
Brahms	Haydn	Schubert
Chopin	Lehar	Vivaldi
Debussy	Liszt	Wagner

Hidden in this grid are 18 names of well-known composers. Can you find them? You can move horizontally, vertically or diagonally and in a forward or backward direction.

Answer see page **84**

41

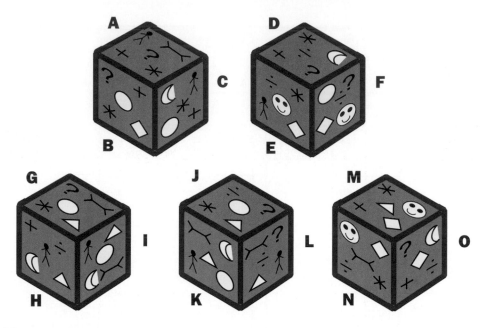

PUZZLE 64

There are two sides on these cubes that contain exactly the same symbols. Can you spot them?

Answer see page **84**

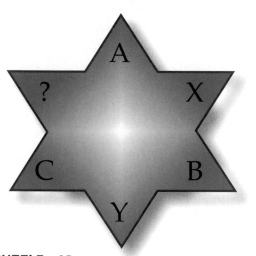

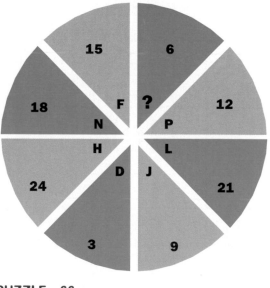

PUZZLE 65

Can you find the letter to complete the sequence starting at A?

Answer see page **84**

PUZZLE 66

The letters and numbers in this wheel are related in some way. Can you find what letter should replace the question mark?

Answer see page **84**

 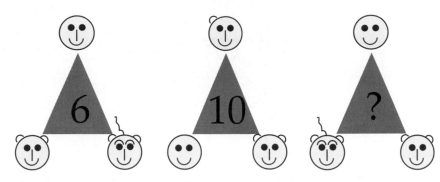

PUZZLE 67

Can you work out what number the
question mark in the triangle stands for?

Answer see page **84**

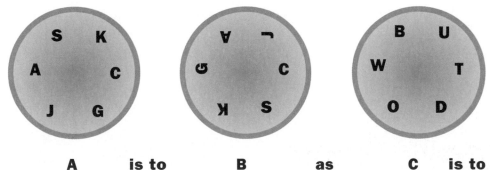

A   is to   B   as   C   is to

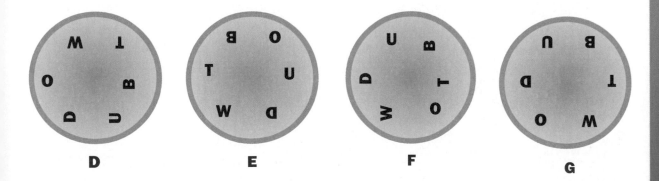

D   E   F   G

PUZZLE 68

Answer see page **84**

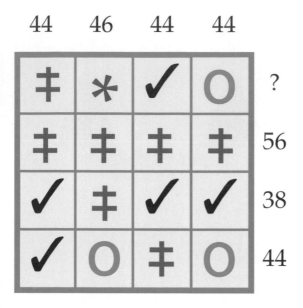

PUZZLE 69

Each symbol in this square represents a number. Can you work out what number should replace the question mark?

Answer see page **84**

PUZZLE 70

In this diagram the mathematical signs (+ and – only) between each letter (which has a value equal to its position in the alphabet) have gone missing.
Can you restore them in a way that you arrive at the letter in the middle of the diamond?

Answer see page **84**

PUZZLE 71

Can you find the two sides on these cubes that contain exactly the same symbols?

Answer see page **84**

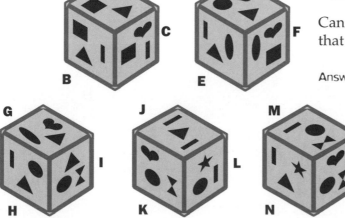

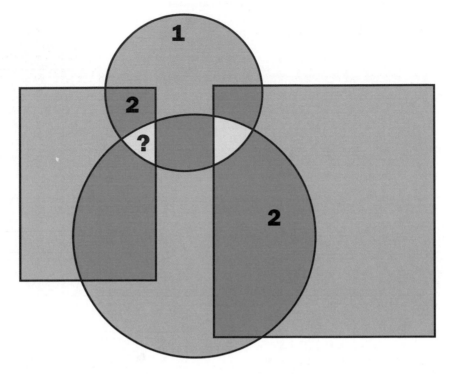

PUZZLE 72

This diagram was constructed according to a certain logic. Can you work out what number should replace the question mark?

Answer see page **84**

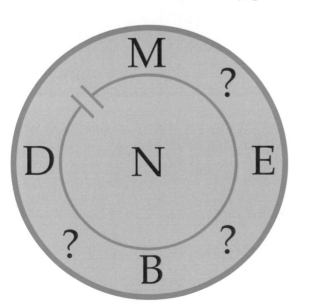

PUZZLE 73

Can you work out whether + or – should replace the question mark to arrive at the letter in the middle of the circle?

Answer see page **84**

 **A**

 **B**

C

D

PUZZLE 74

The symbols in the above grid follow a pattern. Can you work it out and find the missing section?

Answer see page **84**

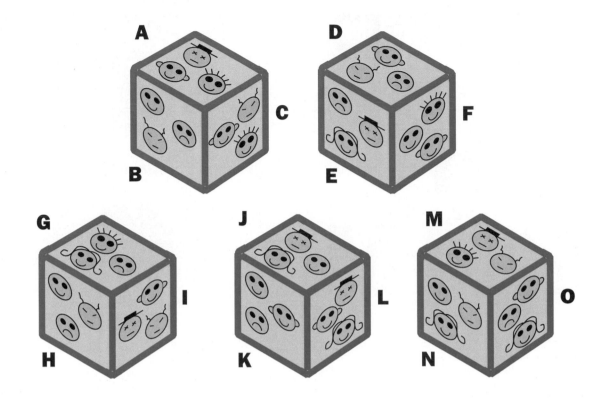

PUZZLE 75

Can you work out which two sides on these cubes contain the same symbols?

Answer see page **84**

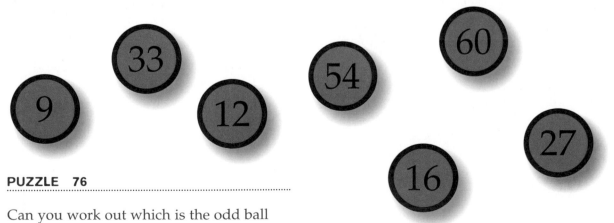

PUZZLE 76

Can you work out which is the odd ball out?

Answer see page **84**

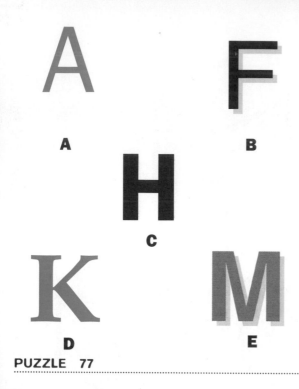

PUZZLE 77

Can you work out which of these letters is the odd one out?

Answer see page **84**

PUZZLE 78

Can you replace the question marks with + or − so that both sections in this diagram add up to the same value?

Answer see page **84**

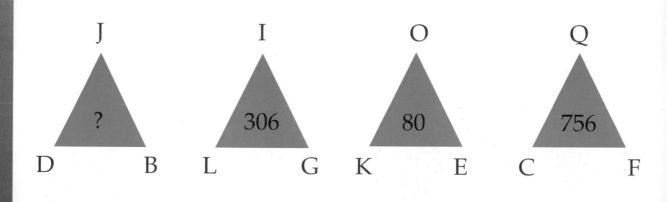

PUZZLE 79

Can you work out what number fits into the first triangle?

Answer see page **85**

A is to B   as   C is to

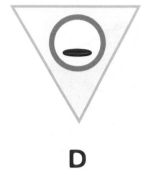

D

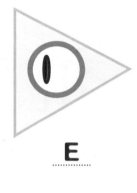

E

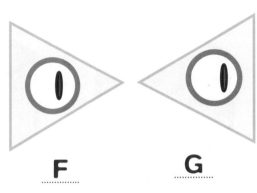

F   G

PUZZLE 80

Answer see page **85**

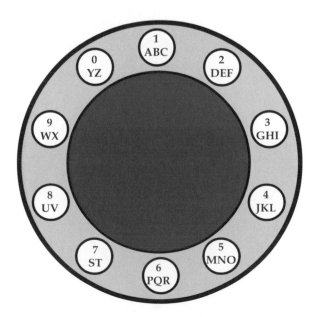

PUZZLE 81

The diagram represents an old-fashioned telephone dial with letters as well as numbers. Below is a list of numbers representing 10 large cities from around the world. Can you use the diagram to decode them?

A: 5151327726   **B:** 3417359

C: 75845872   **D:** 75542574

E: 815158826   **F:** 1153454

G: 11418771   **H:** 52415865

I: 116124551   **J:** 7116152575

Answer see page **85**

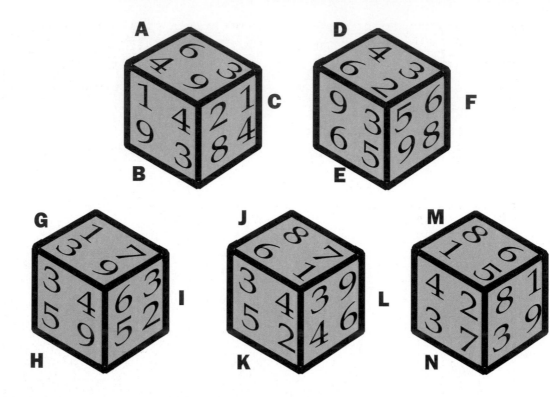

PUZZLE 82

Two sides of these cubes contain exactly
the same numbers.
Can you spot them?

Answer see page **85**

PUZZLE 83

In this diamond the four mathematical
signs +, −, × and ÷ have been left out. Can
you work out which sign fits between each
pair of numbers to arrive at the number in
the middle of the diagram? To start you
off, three of the signs are each used twice.

Answer see page **85**

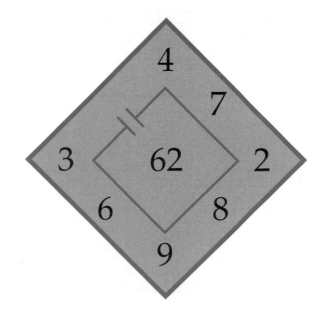

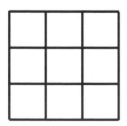

PUZZLE 84

The symbols in this grid follow a pattern. Can you work it out and complete the missing section?

Answer see page **85**

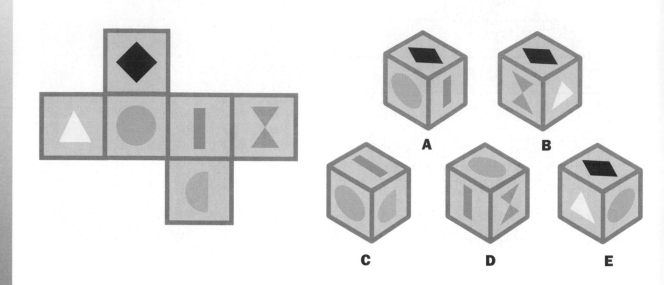

PUZZLE 85

Which of these cubes cannot be made from this layout?

Answer see page **85**

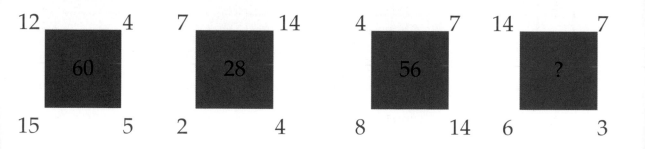

PUZZLE 86

Can you work out the number needed to complete the square?

Answer see page **85**

PUZZLE 87

Can you find the mathematical signs
that should replace the question marks
in this diagram?

Answer see page **85**

PUZZLE 88

Can you crack the logic of this diagram
and replace the question mark
with a number?

Answer see page **85**

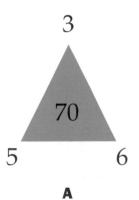

A

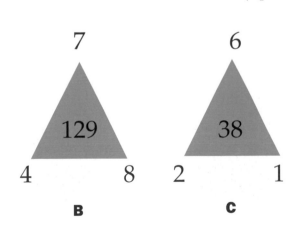

B

C

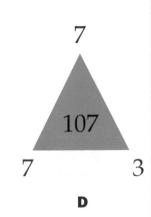

D

PUZZLE 89

The four triangles are linked by a simple
mathematical formula. Can you discover
what it is and then find the odd one out?

Answer see page **85**

PUZZLE 90

These tiles when placed in the right order will form a square in which each horizontal line is identical with one vertical line. Can you successfully form the square?

Answer see page 85

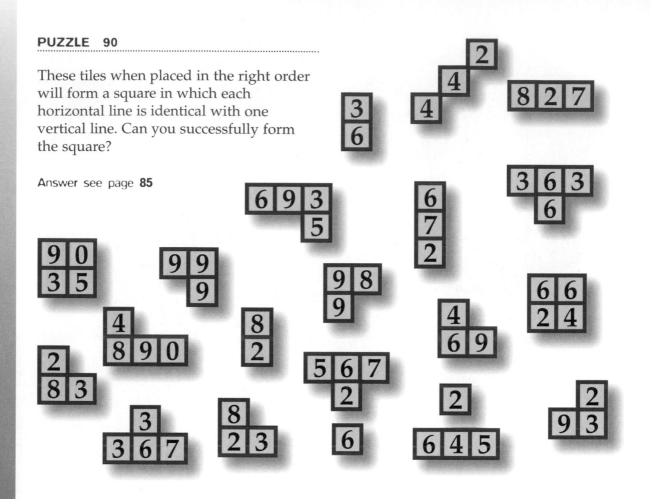

PUZZLE 91

The diagram represents an old-fashioned telephone dial with letters as well as numbers. Below is a list of numbers representing 10 international capital cities. Can you use the diagram to decode them?

Answer see page 85

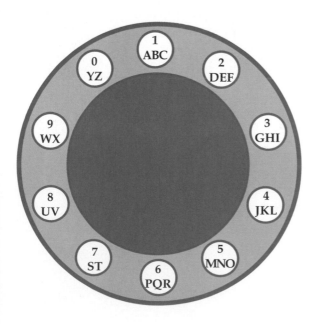

A. 1562531325

B. 661382

C. 455255

D. 126435

E. 75405

F. 157726215

G. 775143545

H. 1545515

I. 512632

J. 154161

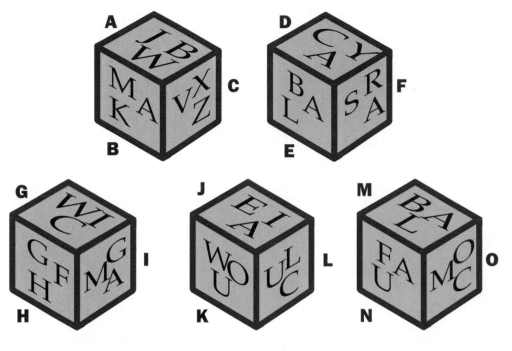

PUZZLE 92

Can you work out which sides on these cubes contain the same letters?

Answer see page **85**

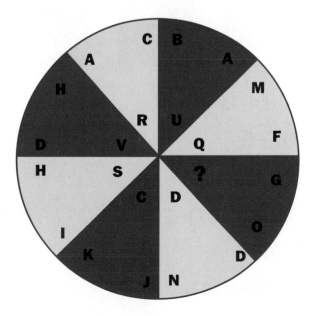

PUZZLE 93

Can you find out what letter completes the wheel?

Answer see page **85**

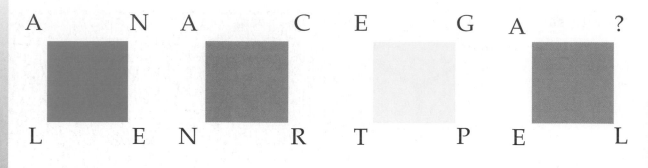

A   N   A   C   E   G   A   ?

L   E   N   R   T   P   E   L

PUZZLE 94

Find the missing letter.

Answer see page **85**

PUZZLE 95

The words can be put in front of the colors to form well-known names or expressions.

Answer see page **86**

BLOOD

DEEP

CODE

TOBACCO

SEA

EMERALD

PUZZLE 96

How would you continue this series?

Answer see page **86**

PUZZLE 97

Can Orange join the other colors?

Answer see page **86**

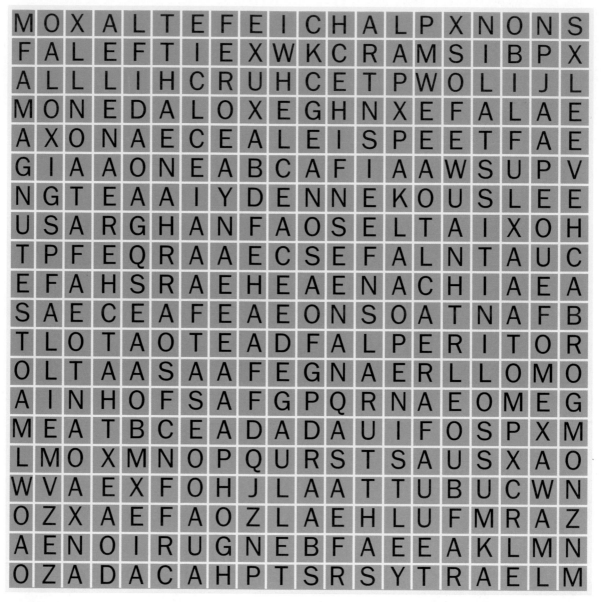

```
M O X A L T E F E I C H A L P X N O N S
F A L E F T I E X W K C R A M S I B P X
A L L L I H C R U H C E T P W O L I J L
M O N E D A L O X E G H N X E F A L A E
A X O N A E C E A L E I S P E E T F A E
G I A A O N E A B C A F I A A W S U P V
N G T E A A I Y D E N N E K O U S L E E
U S A R G H A N F A O S E L T A I X O H
T P F E Q R A A E C S E F A L N T A U C
E F A H S R A E H E A E N A C H I A E A
S A E C E A F E A E O N S O A T N A F B
T L O T A O T E A D F A L P E R I T O R
O L T A A S A A F E G N A E R L L O M O
A I N H O F S A F G P Q R N A E O M E G
M E A T B C E A D A D A U I F O S P X M
L M O X M N O P Q U R S T S A U S X A O
W V A E X F O H J L A A T T U B U C W N
O Z X A E F A O Z L A E H L U F M R A Z
A E N O I R U G N E B F A E E A K L M N
O Z A D A C A H P T S R S Y T R A E L M
```

Arafat

Mussolini

Gorbachev

Bismarck

Pinochet

Lincoln

De Gaulle

Thatcher

Mitterrand

Gandhi

Ben Gurion

Napoleon

Kennedy

Churchill

Stalin

Mao Tse Tung

Franco

Yeltsin

PUZZLE 98

The above grid contains the names of 18 famous statesmen. Can you discover them?

Answer see page 86

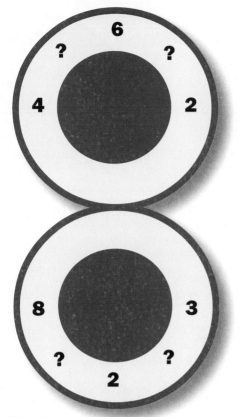

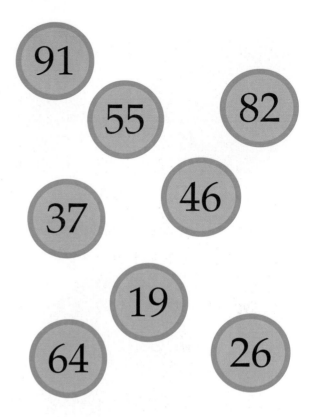

PUZZLE 99

Can you replace the question marks in this diagram with the symbols × and ÷ so that both sections arrive at the same value?

Answer see page **86**

PUZZLE 100

Can you work out which of these balls is the odd one out?

Answer see page **86**

PUZZLE 101

Can you find the missing letter in this star?

Answer see page **86**

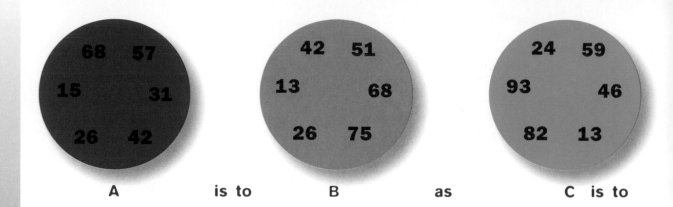

A   is to   B   as   C is to

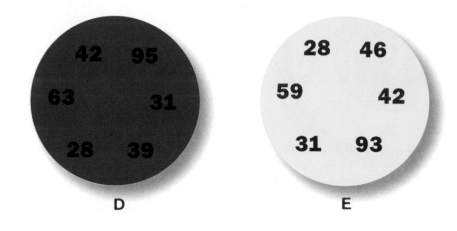

D   E

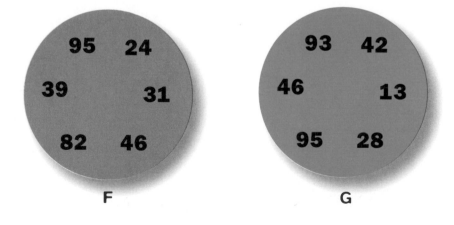

F   G

PUZZLE 102

Answer see page **86**

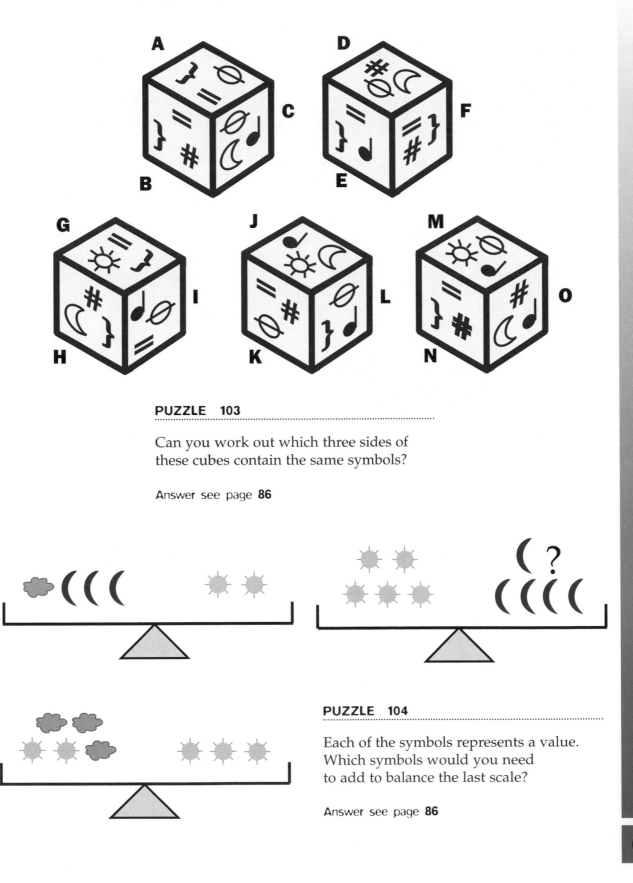

PUZZLE 103

Can you work out which three sides of these cubes contain the same symbols?

Answer see page **86**

PUZZLE 104

Each of the symbols represents a value. Which symbols would you need to add to balance the last scale?

Answer see page **86**

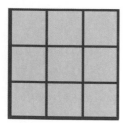

PUZZLE 105

The symbols in this grid behave in a predictable manner.
When you have discovered their sequence it should be possible to fill in the blank segment.

Answer see page **86**

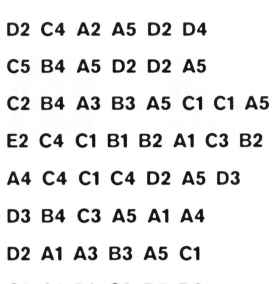

D2 C4 A2 A5 D2 D4

C5 B4 A5 D2 D2 A5

C2 B4 A3 B3 A5 C1 C1 A5

E2 C4 C1 B1 B2 A1 C3 B2

A4 C4 C1 C4 D2 A5 D3

D3 B4 C3 A5 A1 A4

D2 A1 A3 B3 A5 C1

C2 A1 B2 C3 D5 D3

PUZZLE 106

The code produced by this grid is a little more difficult than the last. The coded words to the right of the grid are first names. Can you work them out?

Answer see page **86**

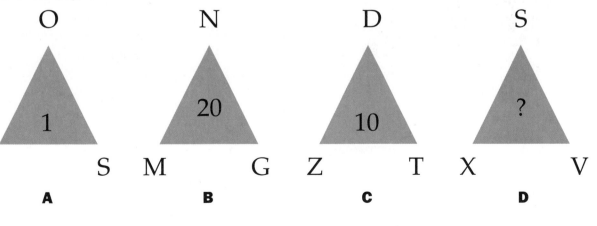

PUZZLE 107

Can you work out the rule these triangles follow and find the missing number?

Answer see page **86**

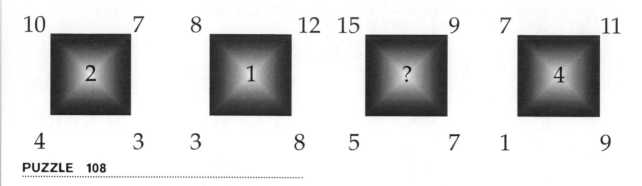

10   7   8   12   15   9   7   11

2   1   ?   4

4   3   3   8   5   7   1   9

PUZZLE 108

Can you work out what number should replace the question mark in the square?

Answer see page **87**

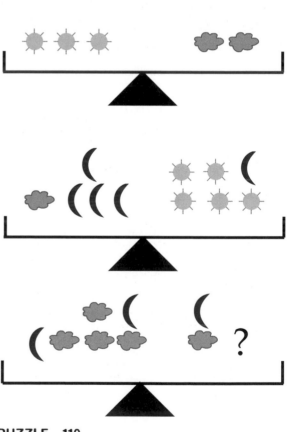

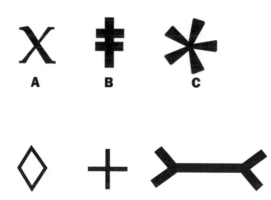

A   B   C

D   E   F

PUZZLE 109

Can you find the odd one out of these symbols?

Answer see page **87**

PUZZLE 110

Can you work out which symbols should replace the question mark, so that the scales balance?

Answer see page **87**

PUZZLE 111

Can you find the letter that would
complete the star?

Answer see page **87**

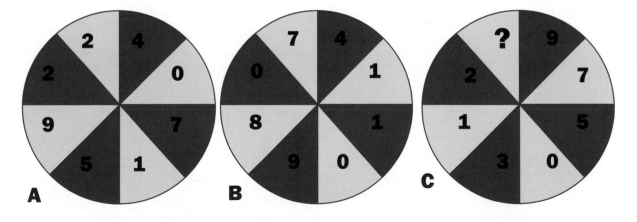

A

B

C

PUZZLE 112

Can you work out what number should
replace the question mark to follow the
rules of the other wheels?

Answer see page **87**

PUZZLE 113

The two pictures are very similar but not quite identical. Find 10 ways in which A differs from B.

Answer see page **87**

A

B

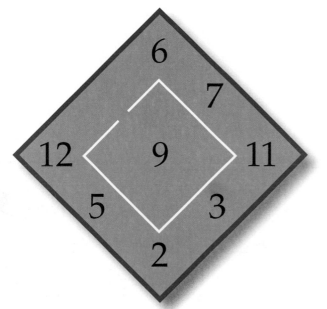

PUZZLE 114

In this diagram, starting from the top of the diamond and working in a clockwise direction, the four basic mathematical signs (+, −, ×, ÷) have been omitted. Your task is to restore them so that the calculation, with answer in the middle, is correct.

Answer see page **87**

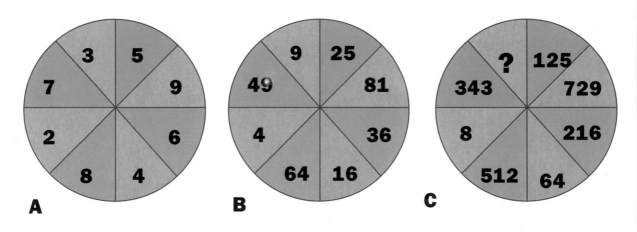

A   B   C

PUZZLE 115

A curious logic governs the numbers in these circles. Can you discover what it is and then work out what the missing number should be?

Answer see page **87**

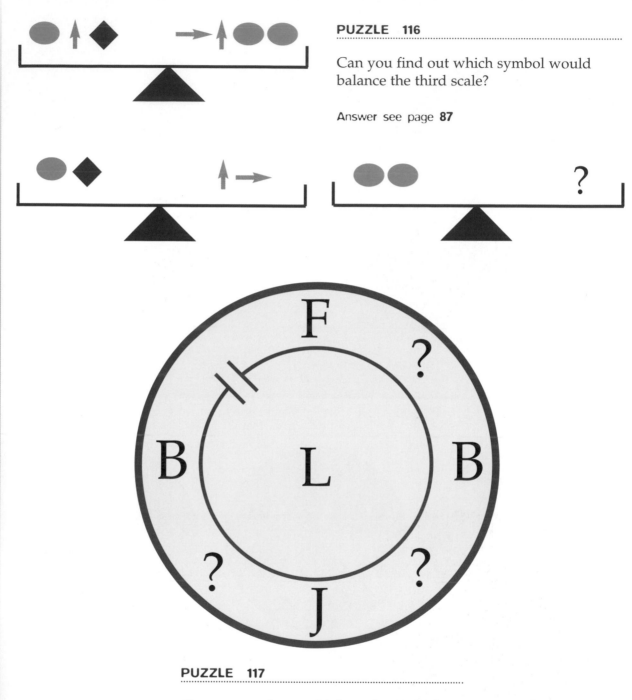

PUZZLE 116

Can you find out which symbol would balance the third scale?

Answer see page **87**

PUZZLE 117

Can you work out which mathematical signs should replace the question marks in this diagram? You have a choice between − or +.

Answer see page **87**

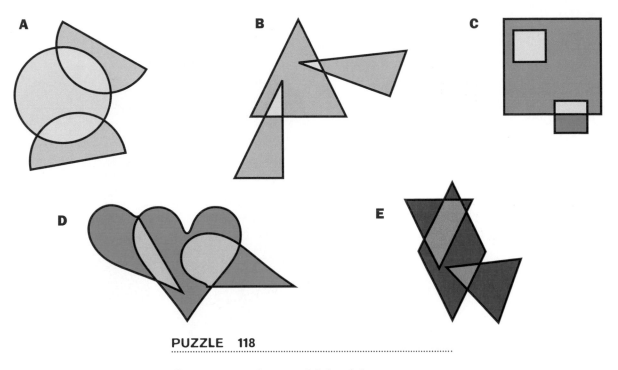

A

B

C

D

E

PUZZLE 118

Can you work out which of these diagrams is different from the others?

Answer see page **87**

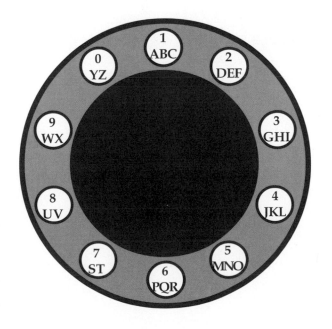

PUZZLE 119

The diagram represents an old-fashioned telephone dial with letters as well as numbers. Below is a list of numbers representing 10 American towns or cities. Can you decode them?

Answer see page **87**

A. 214417

B. 7217742

C. 1331135

D. 534918422

E. 53552165437

F. 65674152

G. 2276537

H. 1741571

I. 1351355173

J. 352315165437

PUZZLE 120

Can you work out what the blank clockface should look like?

Answer see page **87**

35   47   38   24

‡	✳	✳	✳	?
✓	‡	‡	✓	40
✓	O	✓	✓	21
O	O	O	O	48

PUZZLE 121

Can you work out what number each symbol represents and find the value of the question mark?

Answer see page **87**

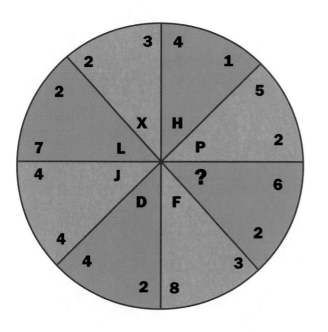

PUZZLE 122

Can you unravel the reasoning behind this diagram and find the correct letter to replace the question mark?

Answer see page 87

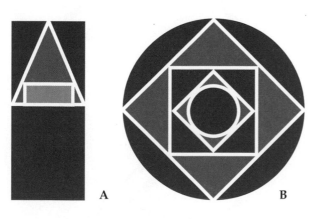

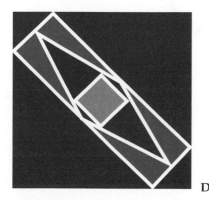

PUZZLE 123

Which is the odd one out?

Answer see page 87

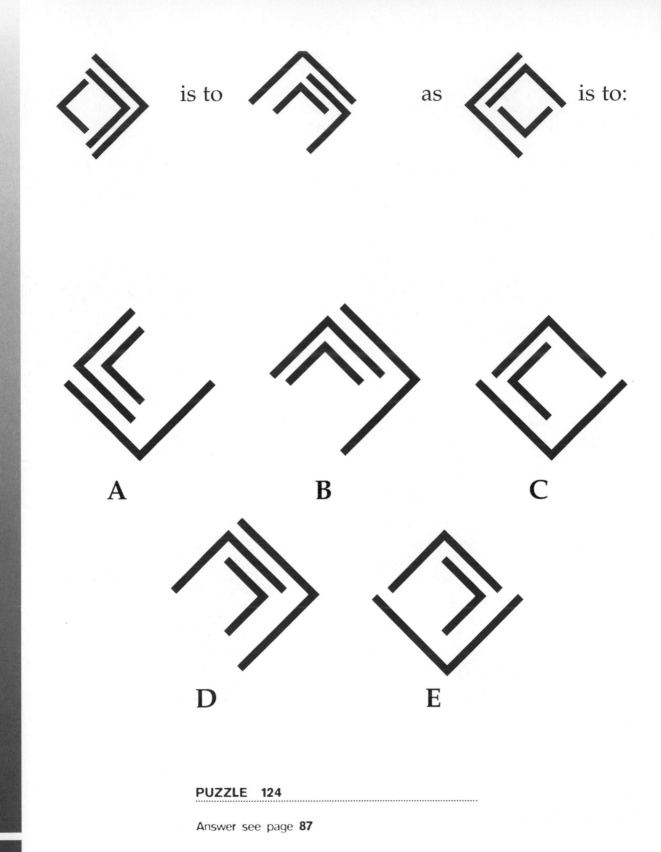

is to ... as ... is to:

A

B

C

D

E

PUZZLE   124

Answer see page **87**

PUZZLE 125

Which of the following shapes forms a
perfect triangle when combined with the
picture on the right ?

Answer see page **87**

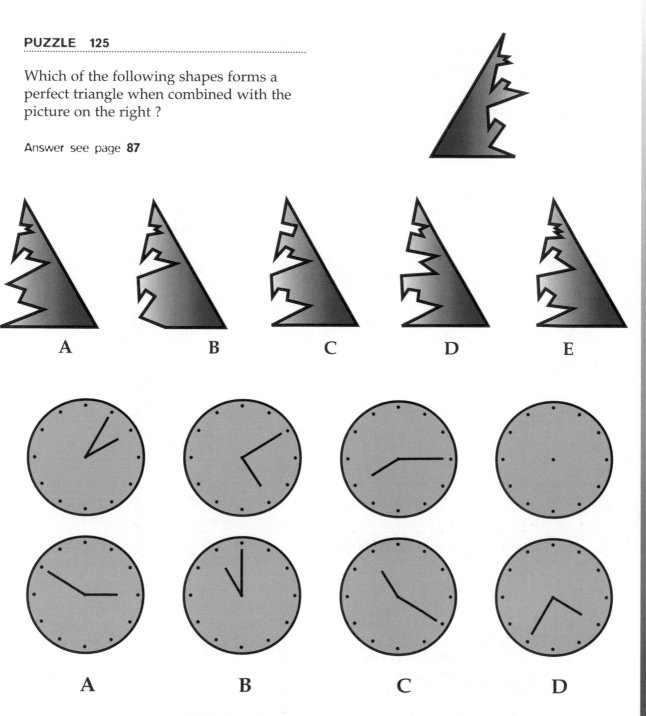

A   B   C   D   E

A   B   C   D

PUZZLE 126

Look at the clock faces shown in the top
line above. Choose one from the second
row to continue the series.

Answer see page **87**

PUZZLE 127

Which is the odd one out?

Answer see page **87**

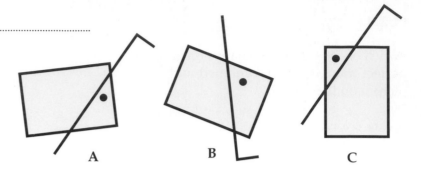

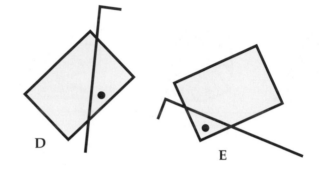

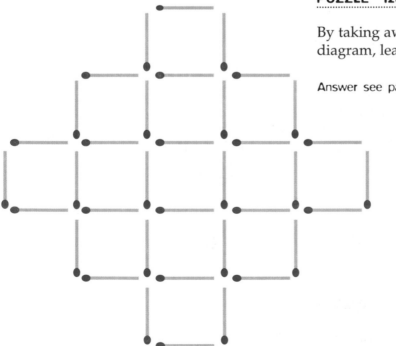

PUZZLE 128

By taking away four matches from this diagram, leave eight small squares.

Answer see page **88**

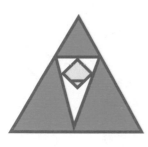 is to  as

is to:

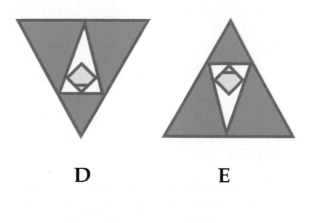

A   B   C

D   E

PUZZLE 129

Answer see page **88**

   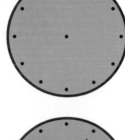

A   B   C   D   E

PUZZLE 130

Which is the odd one out?

Answer see page **88**

A   **B**   **C**   **D**

PUZZLE 131

Another series of clock faces. Again it is up to you to work out the logic behind the series in the top row and pick the clock from the bottom row that replaces the blank clock.

Answer see page **88**

A   is to   B   as   C   is to:

D   E   F

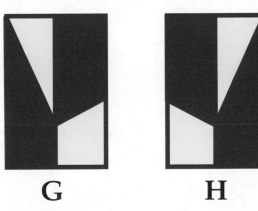

G   H

PUZZLE   132

Answer see page **88**

PUZZLE 133

Someone has made a mistake decorating
this cake. Can you correct the pattern?

Answer see page **88**

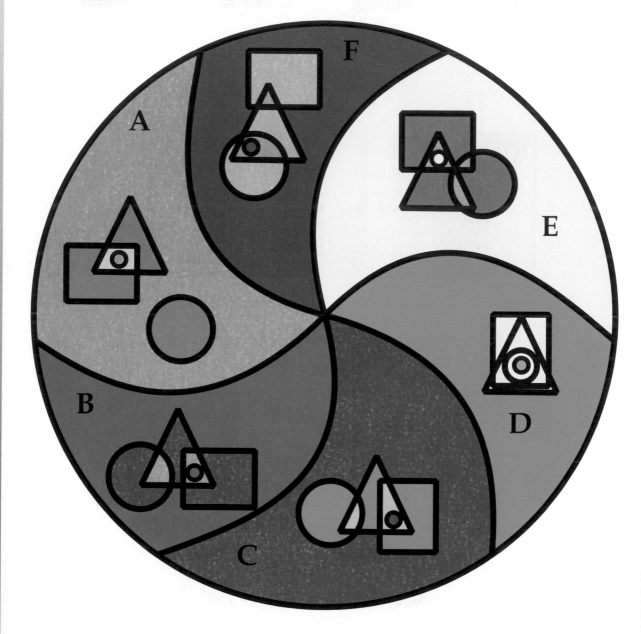

PUZZLE 134

Which of the following comes next in the sequence?

Answer see page **88**

A   B   C

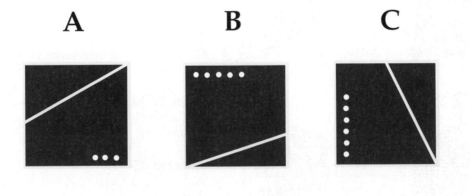

D   E

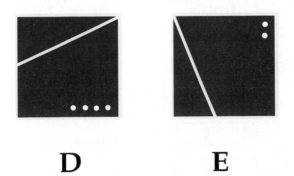

Answer 1
E. In all the others the colors follow the same sequence: light blue, red, dark blue, green, yellow, pink.

Answer 2
Rob Roy: Red Orange Blue, Red, Orange, Yellow

Answer 3
Brown. Letters in the names of opposite pairs of colors always add up to 10 (eg, Pink, four letters, and Yellow, six letters, make 10).

Answer 4
A. Pattern is: 2 by arch on top, 4 by arch at right, 3 by arch on bottom, 2 by arch at left. Start at the top left corner and move down the grid in vertical lines, reverting to the top of the next column when you reach the bottom.

Answer 5
E.

Answer 6
4. Multiply the two numbers in the outer circle of each segment and place the product in the inner circle two segments away in a clockwise direction.

Answer 7

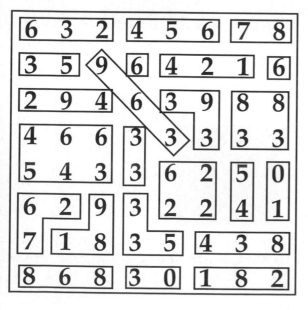

Answer 8
4. The number relates to the number of shapes in which the number is enclosed.

Answer 9
7. Add the three numbers at the corner of each triangle, multiply by 2, and place that number in the middle.

Answer 10
8. Starting at H, and working clockwise, subtract the value of second letter, based on its value in the alphabet, from the value of the first letter, and put sum in following corner.

Answer 11
21. Add all the numbers of each triangle together and place the sum in the middle of next triangle. When you reach D put the sum in A.

Answer 12
15. None of the other numbers have a divisor.

Answer 13
1:00. The minute hand moves forward 20 minutes, the hour hand moves back 1 hour.

Answer 14
A diamond. (4 diamonds = 3 left-arrows = 6 up-arrows)

Answer 15
A.	California	F.	Oregon
B.	Texas	G.	Virginia
C.	Nebraska	H.	Florida
D.	Alaska	I.	Colorado
E.	Idaho	J.	Arizona

Answer 16
F. The symbols are reflected over a vertical line.

Answer 17
E. It contains no curved lines.

Answer 18
G. Add 2 lines to the body, take away 1, add 3, take away 2, add 4, take away 3.

Answer 19

6:45. The minute hand moves back 15, 30 and 45 minutes. The hour hand moves forward 3, 6 and 9 hours.

Answer 20

10. Replace each letter by the value of its position in the alphabet. Start at E and add 1, then 2, then 3, then 4, then 5, then 1, then 2 etc. When you reach 26 (Z), go back to 1 (A).

Answer 21

Pink. All the other colors are either primary or secondary colors. Pink is a hue.

Answer 22

D. The letters form five-letter words when you include the first letter of the color in the square: baGel, cuPid, adObe, idYll.

Answer 23

Below, because it has only one syllable.

Answer: 24

No, it has no 'e' in it.

Answer 25

Blue Moon. Pink Champagne. White Gold. Yellow Submarine. Purple Rain. Orange City.

Answer 26

The order is 2 +, 3 −, 2 ÷, 3 x. The puzzle goes in an inward clockwise spiral starting from the top left corner.

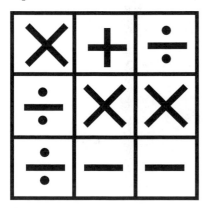

Answer 27

D and L.

Answer 28

19. Starting from D, each number, or its alphabetic equivalent, advances three.

Answer 29

39. Tick = 6, star = 9, cross = 3, O = 24.

Answer 30

E and O. The letters are N, O, P and X.

Answer 31

Q. The letters are in the following alphabetical order: miss one, miss two, miss three, miss one etc.

Answer 32

Austen	Hemingway
Michener	Chaucer
Huxley	Orwell
Chekov	Ibsen
Proust	Dickens
Kafka	Tolstoy
Flaubert	Kipling
Twain	Goethe
Lawrence	Zola

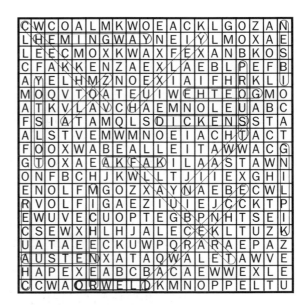

Answer 33

B. The number of sides of the internal figures should increase by one each time. B is the odd one out because its internal figures should have 2 sides.

Answer 34
R. Multiply the value of the three earliest letters, based on their value in the alphabet, by 2. The answer goes in the opposite triangle. I (9) x 2 = 18 (R).

Answer 35

Answer 36
6:20. The minute hand advances 20 minutes each time, the hour hand goes back 2 hours each time.

Answer 37
8. Add all the numbers together. In a yellow square you add 5 to the sum, in a green one you subtract 5.

Answer 38
Taking first letters of the colors you will get the letters to form POPPY.

Answer 39
None. The number of letters rises by one each time. There is no 7-letter color in the spectrum.

Answer 40
C. In all other cases the first letters of the colors form words: gory, poor, prop, orgy.

Answer 41
Picasso, Rembrandt, Gaugin, Leonardo, Constable, Raphael, Van Gogh, Matisse.
A = 1:4; B = 1:3; C = 1:2; D = 1:1; E = 2:4, etc.

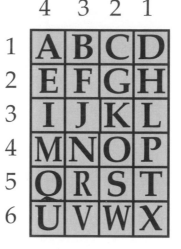

Answer 42
68. Square = 7; X = 11; Z = 3; Heart = 17.

Answer 43
72. Multiply all the numbers in the top sections to arrive at the number in the opposite bottom section. Multiply by 3 in the first circle, by 6 in the second one, and by 9 in the third circle.

Answer 44
C.

Answer 45
Start at the top right corner and work in a clockwise inward spiral. The pattern is: two ticks, one heart, two faces, one tick, two hearts, one face, etc.

Answer 46
One cloud. The values are: Cloud = 3; Umbrella = 2; Moon = 4.

Answer 47

C. It has an odd number of elements, the others all have an even number.

Answer 48

S. Look at opposite triangles. D is 4th letter of the alphabet, W is 4th from the end. F is 6th letter, while U is 6th from the end. H is the 8th letter, thus the missing letter is the one which is 8th from the end.

Answer 49

Top half: ÷ x; bottom half: x x.

Answer 50

A full circle. Go first along the top of the triangles, then along the bottoms. Each circle is filled one-quarter at a time until the circle is complete, then reverts to one-quarter filled.

Answer 51

33. Star = 8; Tick = 12; Cross = 13; Circle = 5.

Answer 52

E and I.

Answer 53

– – x.

Answer 54

C. The letters represent values based on their position in the alphabet. They represent the number of straight-sided figures in which they are enclosed. The circle is a red herring.

Answer 55

Jane Asher
Julia Roberts
Mel Gibson
Julie Christie
Meryl Streep
Paul Newman
Jane Fonda
Gene Wilder

Richard Gere
Michael Caine
Brooke Shields
Dustin Hoffman
Tom Cruise
Emma Thompson
Robert Redford
Jodie Foster

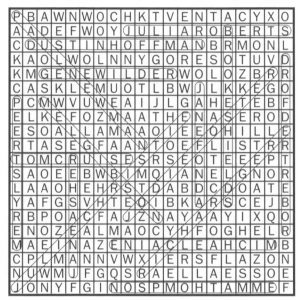

Answer 56

A. Add one new element to the face, then add one hair and an element to the face, then a hair, then a hair and an element to the face, repeat sequence.

Answer 57

15. Start at the top left corner and add that number to each corner in a clockwise direction, eg. 7 + 7 = 14 + 7 = 21 + 7 = 28 + 7 = 35.

Answer 58

Answer 59
Five suns. Moons = 2; Cloud = 3; Sun = 4.

Answer 60
G. The internal patterns are rotated 180°.

Answer 61
C and K.

Answer 62
23. Square = 9; Cross = 5; Z = 6; Heart = 7.

Answer 63

Bach	Dvorak
Mendelssohn	Beethoven
Grieg	Mozart
Borodin	Handel
Purcell	Brahms
Haydn	Schubert
Chopin	Lehar
Vivaldi	Debussy
Liszt	Wagner

K	L	N	B	C	E	W	O	P	Q	B	A	I	K	M	O	L	C
G	A	E	C	C	W	V	R	A	E	I	X	C	M	O	L	A	D
B	E	F	H	A	E	L	E	H	A	R	U	O	H	N	K	M	X
O	A	B	A	C	H	A	N	A	E	X	T	A	T	O	T	E	W
R	L	O	N	E	F	A	G	E	T	W	Y	A	E	X	P	M	M
O	N	A	D	E	A	G	A	H	A	D	H	E	L	L	E	I	E
D	A	C	E	F	G	E	W	A	N	E	A	E	I	M	C	O	N
I	U	F	L	I	S	Z	T	B	E	N	T	V	O	W	L	C	D
N	A	E	K	M	O	Z	G	A	V	E	A	Z	C	K	L	P	E
Q	S	K	A	E	K	E	B	E	O	H	A	R	T	U	E	K	L
L	W	A	A	E	I	P	Q	R	H	R	A	E	T	X	C	K	S
A	C	E	I	R	V	O	S	P	T	Q	V	R	W	B	R	C	S
S	D	A	G	E	O	K	W	O	E	L	X	N	M	N	U	T	O
M	O	V	X	Z	K	V	M	N	E	K	E	C	V	A	P	J	H
H	L	W	X	Q	W	A	D	E	B	U	S	S	Y	A	T	O	N
A	O	W	P	X	B	E	I	E	P	Q	O	Z	A	C	L	T	W
R	A	C	A	S	C	H	U	B	E	R	T	T	O	R	H	D	A
B	B	C	F	K	L	M	N	T	A	C	T	O	A	R	Z	W	L

Answer 64
I and K. The figures are: matchstick man, triangle, half-moon, circle, stile.

Answer 65
Z. Take the value of the letters, based on their position in the alphabet. A back 3 is X; X forward 4 is B; B back 3 is Y; Y forward 4 is C, etc.

Answer 66
B. The numerical value of each letter in the alphabet is two-thirds of the number in the opposite segment.

Answer 67
2. The faces represent numbers, based on the elements in or around the face (excluding the head). Multiply the top number with the bottom right number and divide by the bottom left number. Place the answer in the middle.

Answer 68
D. Letters with only curves stay the same, letters with curves and straight lines turn by 90° and letters with only straight lines by 180°.

Answer 69
40. Star = 7; Tick = 8; Cross = 14; Circle = 11.

Answer 70
$F + I + E - J + N - W + H = I$.

Answer 71
K and O.

Answer 72
3. The numbers refer to the number of shapes that surround each digit.

Answer 73
$M - E + B + D = N$.

Answer 74
B. Start from top left corner and move in a vertical boustrophedon. Order is: 4 smiley face, 1 sad face, 3 straight mouth, 2 face with hair, etc.

Answer 75
B and H.

Answer 76
16. All the other numbers can be divided by 3.

Answer 77
D. Only the K has serifs.

Answer 78
Top half: + +; bottom half: + −.

Answer 79
825. Multiply the value of the letters, based on their value in the alphabet, from each triangle and place the product in the next but one triangle to the right.

Answer 80
E. Turn the diagram by 90° clockwise.

Answer 81
A. Manchester F. Bangkok
B. Glasgow G. Calcutta
C. Toulouse H. Melbourne
D. Smolensk I. Barcelona
E. Vancouver J. Sacramento

Answer 82
A and L. The numbers are 3, 4, 6 and 9.

Answer 83
$4 \times 7 \div 2 + 8 + 9 \times 6 \div 3 = 62$.

Answer 84
Start at top left corner and move in a vertical boustrophedon. The order is two hearts, one square root, two crossed circles, one cross, one heart, two square roots, one crossed circle, two crosses, etc.

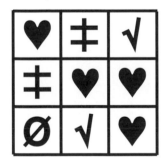

Answer 85
D.

Answer 86
42. Take the number in the middle of the square, divide it by the number in the top left corner and place the new number in the bottom right corner. Again take the middle number, but now divide it by the number in the top right corner and place this new number in the bottom left corner.

Answer 87
$5 \times 4 \div 2 + 7 = 17$.

Answer 88
2. Relates to the number of shapes that enclose each figure.

Answer 89
C. The number in the middle is the sum of the squares of the numbers at the points of the triangles. C does not fit this pattern.

Answer 90

Answer 91
Copenhagen, Prague, London, Berlin, Tokyo, Amsterdam, Stockholm, Colombo, Madrid, Ankara.

Answer 92
E and M.

Answer 93
L. Add the value of the two letters in each outer segment, based on their position in the alphabet, and place the answer letter in the opposite inner segment.

Answer 94
P. Each square gives a five-letter word if you include the first letter of the color: anGel, acOrn, egYpt, apPle.

Answer 95
Emerald green, Sea blue, Code Red, Blood orange, Tobacco brown, Deep Purple (pop group)

Answer 96
Indigo and Violet (colors of the rainbow).

Answer 97
No, it starts with a vowel.

Answer 98
Arafat	Gandhi
Mussolini	Ben Gurion
Gorbachev	Napoleon
Bismarck	Kennedy
Pinochet	Churchill
Lincoln	Stalin
De Gaulle	Mao Tse Tung
Thatcher	Franco
Mitterand	Yeltsin

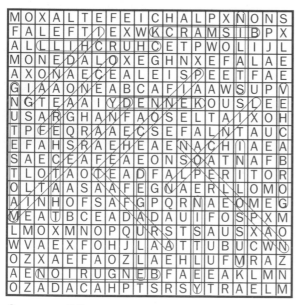

Answer 99
Top half: x ÷; bottom half: ÷ x.

Answer 100
26. The digits in each of the other balls add up to 10.

Answer 101
Q. Reading clockwise from the top, numbers correspond to the alphabetic position of the following letter.

Answer 102
F. The numbers made up of odd numbers are reversed.

Answer 103
B, F and N.

Answer 104
4 moons. Sun = 9; Moon = 5; Cloud = 3.

Answer 105
The pattern is a horizontal boustrophedon starting at the top left. The sequence is: 3 stars, 2 circles, 2, squares, 3 crosses, 2 stars, 3 circles, 3 squares, 2 crosses, etc.

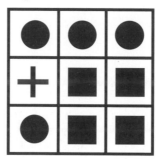

Answer 106
Robert, Pierre, Michelle, Wolfgang, Dolores, Sinead, Rachel, Magnus.

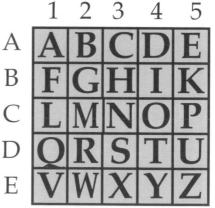

Answer 107
21. Find the value of each letter based on its position in the alphabet, then add the values of the top and left corner together. Subtract the bottom right corner from this number and place the new value in the middle of the triangle.

Answer 108
8. Subtract the bottom left corner from the top left corner. Now subtract the bottom right corner from the top right corner, then subtract this answer from the first difference and put the number in the middle.

Answer 109
The diamond. It is a closed shape.

Answer 110
Three clouds and a moon. Sun = 6; Moon = 7; Cloud = 9.

Answer 111
A. Based on the alphabet, starting at B miss 2 letters, then 3, then 4, etc.

Answer 112
3. The numbers in each wheel add up to 30.

Answer 113

Answer 114
$6 + 7 + 11 \div 3 \times 2 + 5 - 12 = 9$.

Answer 115
27. A number in the first circle is squared and the product is put in the corresponding segment of the second circle. The original number is then cubed and that product is put in the corresponding segment of the third circle.

Answer 116
One arrow pointing up. Oval=1, Arrow=2, Diamond =3

Answer 117
$F - B + J - B = L$.

Answer 118
C. In the others the small shapes added together result in the large shape.

Answer 119
A. Dallas
B. Seattle
C. Chicago
D. Milwaukee
E. Minneapolis
F. Portland
G. Detroit
H. Atlanta
I. Cincinnati
J. Indianapolis

Answer 120
6:50. The minute hand moves back 5, 10 and 15 minutes, while the hour hand moves forward 1, 2 and 3 hours.

Answer 121
35. Star = 6; Tick = 3; Cross = 17; Circle = 12.

Answer 122
N. Multiply the two numbers in each segment. Their product is used to represent a letter (based on its numerical position in the alphabet). This letter is put in the segment diametrically opposite the original numbers.

Answer 123
C. In all other cases, the biggest shape is also the smallest.

Answer 124
C. The smallest segment is rotated 90 degrees clockwise. The middle segment remains static. Largest segment rotated 90° counterclockwise.

Answer 125
B

Answer 126
C. The minute hand moves forward 5 minutes and the hour hand moves forward 3 hours.

Answer 127
B. There is no triangle intersection on the odd one.

Answer 128

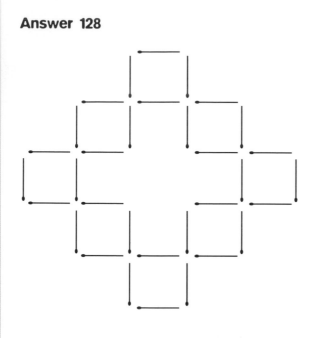

Answer 129
E. Largest shape is reflected horizontally and the size order is reversed.

Answer 130
B. In all other cases the smaller circle is within the larger circle.

Answer 131
B. The minute hand moves back 15 minutes and the hour hand moves forward 3 hours.

Answer 132
H.

Answer 133
F is wrong. In all the others the dot is in both the rectangle and the triangle.

Answer 134
B. The sequence here is minus one dot, plus two dots; the box rotates one place clockwise for each dot added or subtracted.

Medium Puzzles

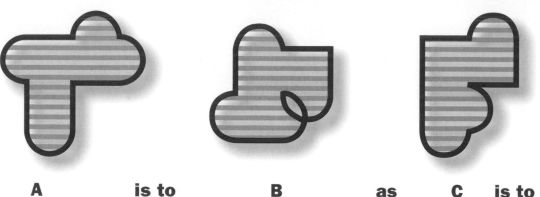

A   is to   B   as   C   is to

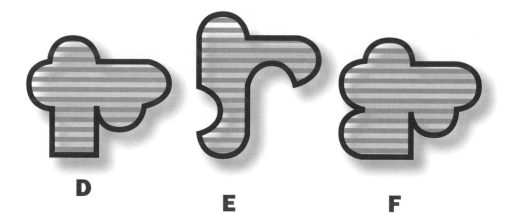

D   E   F

G   H

PUZZLE   135

Answer see page **164**

PUZZLE 136

Can you find the odd shape out?

Answer see page **164**

A

B

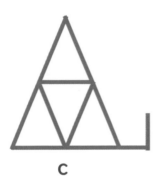

C

D

E

PUZZLE 137

To which of these diagrams could you add a single straight line to match the conditions of the topmost figure?

Answer see page **164**

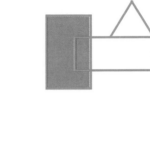

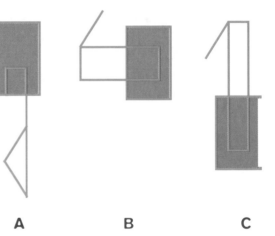

A   B   C

D   E

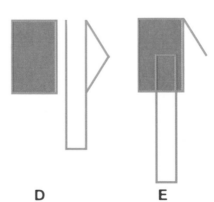

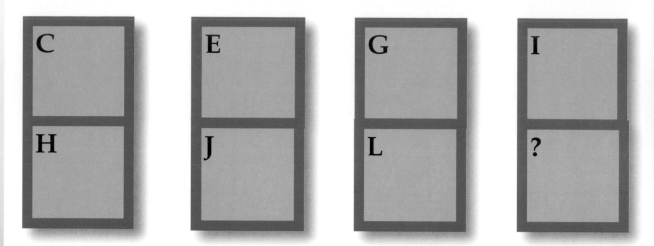

PUZZLE 138

Can you unravel the logic behind these domino pieces and fill in the missing letter?

Answer see page **164**

PUZZLE 139

The four main mathematical signs have been left out of this equation. Can you replace them?

Answer see page **164**

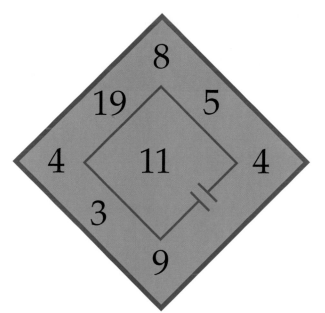

PUZZLE 140

All the suitcases are shown with their destinations. Which is the odd one out?

Answer see page **164**

A. Los Angeles   B. Dallas   C. Houston   D. Kansas   E. Chicago

PUZZLE 141

Can you find the shape that should replace the question mark ?

Answer see page **164**

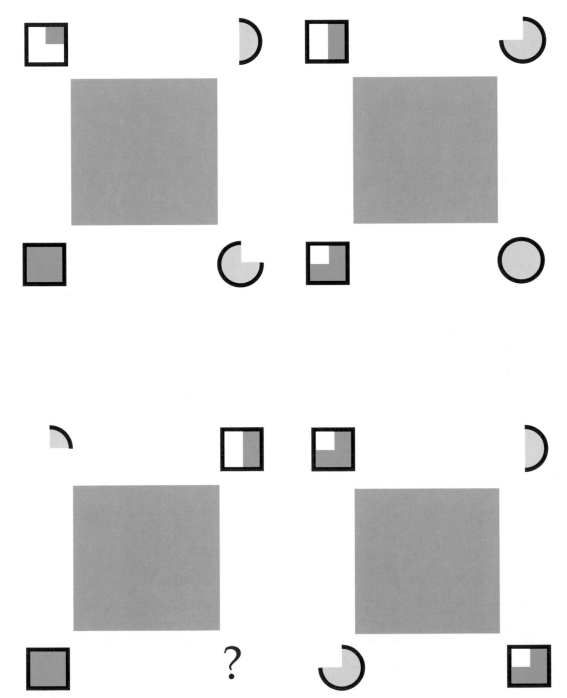

PUZZLE 142

Answer see page **164**

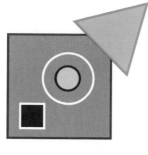  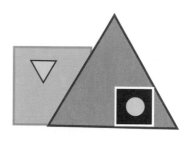

A   **is to**   **B**   **as**   **C**   **is to**

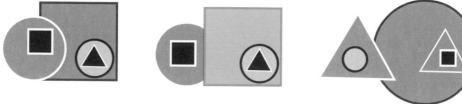

D   **E**   **F**

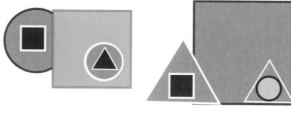

G   **H**

PUZZLE 143

Pick up one letter from each bulb in numerical order. Repeat 4 times. You should find the names of five US states and two dummy letters. What are they?

Answer see page **164**

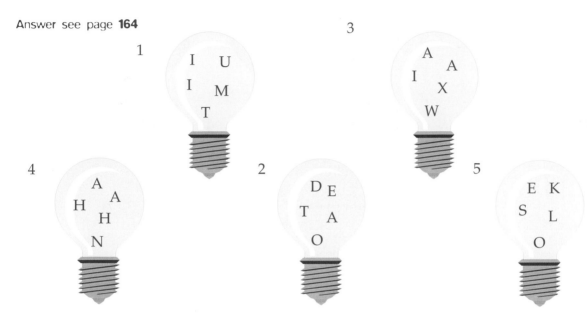

PUZZLE 144

Can you spot the cube that cannot be made from the layout below?

Answer see page **164**

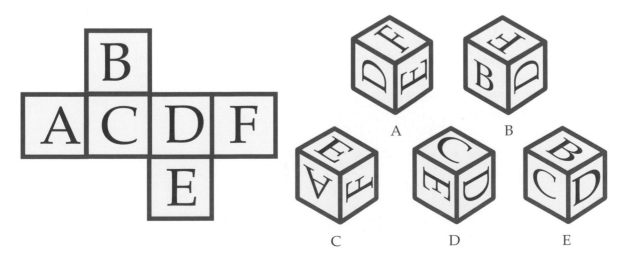

PUZZLE 145

Can you work out which number the missing hand on clock 4 should point to?

Answer see page **164**

1   2

3   4

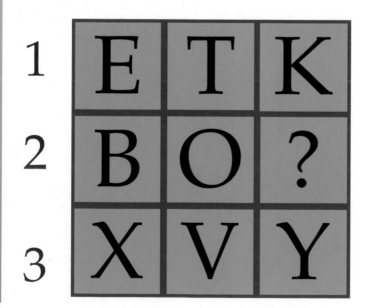

PUZZLE 146

Can you unravel the logic behind this square and find the missing letter?

Answer see page **164**

Z	R	T	T	U	W	W	Z	Z	S	Z	R	T	T	U	W
S	Z	Z	W	W	U	T	T	R	Z	S	Z	Z	W	W	U
Z	S	Z	R	T	T	U	W	W	Z	Z	S	Z	R	T	T
Z	W	W	U	T	T	R	Z	S	Z	Z	W	W	U	T	T
W	Z	Z	S	Z	R	T	T			Z	Z	S	Z	R	
W	U	T	T	R	Z	S	Z		U	T	T	R	Z		
U	W	W	Z	Z	S	Z	R		W	W	Z	Z	S		
T	T	R	Z	S	Z	Z	W	W	U	T	T	R	Z	S	Z
T	T	U	W	W	Z	Z	S	Z	R	T	T	U	W	W	Z
R	Z	S	Z	Z	W	W	U	T	T	R	Z	S	Z	Z	W
Z	R	T	T	U	W	W	Z	Z	S	Z	R	T	T	U	W
S	Z	Z	W	W	U	T	T	R	Z	S	Z	Z	W	W	U
Z	S	Z	R	T	T	U	W	W	Z	Z	S	Z	R	T	T
Z	W	W	U	T	T	R	Z	S	Z	Z	W	W	U	T	T
W	Z	Z	S	Z	R	T	T	U	W	W	Z	Z	S	Z	R
W	U	T	T	R	Z	S	Z	Z	W	W	U	T	T	R	Z

PUZZLE 147

Can you spot the pattern of this grid and complete the missing section?

Answer see page **164**

PUZZLE 148

Can you work out which diagram is the odd one out?

Answer see page **164**

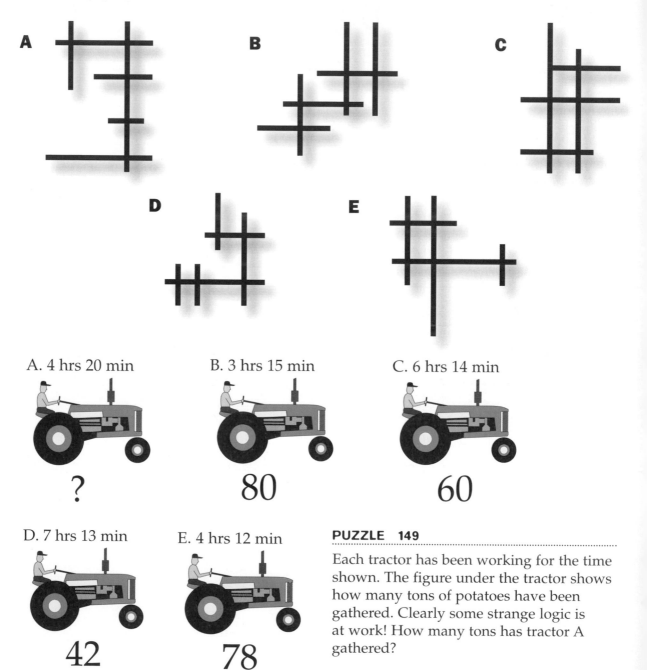

A. 4 hrs 20 min

?

B. 3 hrs 15 min

80

C. 6 hrs 14 min

60

D. 7 hrs 13 min

42

E. 4 hrs 12 min

78

PUZZLE 149

Each tractor has been working for the time shown. The figure under the tractor shows how many tons of potatoes have been gathered. Clearly some strange logic is at work! How many tons has tractor A gathered?

Answer see page **164**

PUZZLE 150

Answer see page **164**

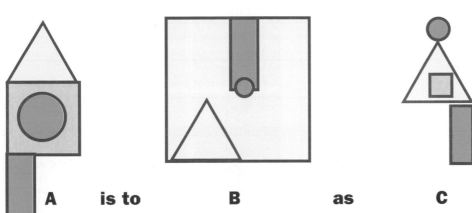

A   is to   B   as   C   is to

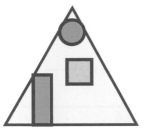

D   E   F

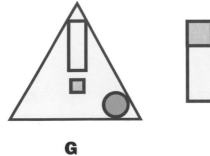

G   H

PUZZLE 151

Can you work out the logic behind this square and complete the missing section?

Answer see page **164**

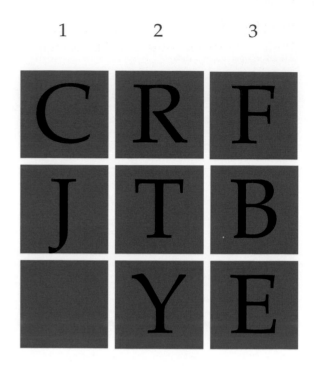

1   2   3

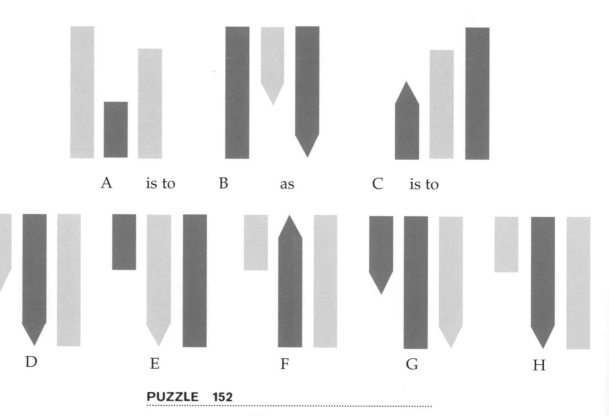

A   is to   B   as   C   is to

D   E   F   G   H

PUZZLE 152

Answer see page **164**

PUZZLE 153

Which of these layouts could be used to make the cube to the right?

Answer see page **165**

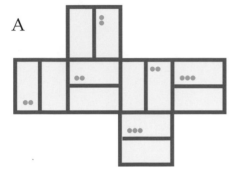

A

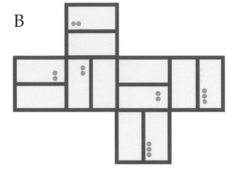

B

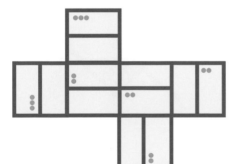

C

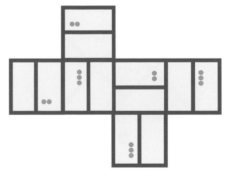

D

E

PUZZLE 154

Answer see page **165**

 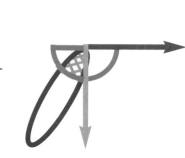 

A   **is to**   **B**   **as**   **C**   **is to**

D   **E**

F   **G**

PUZZLE 155

Can you find the odd shape out?

Answer see page **165**

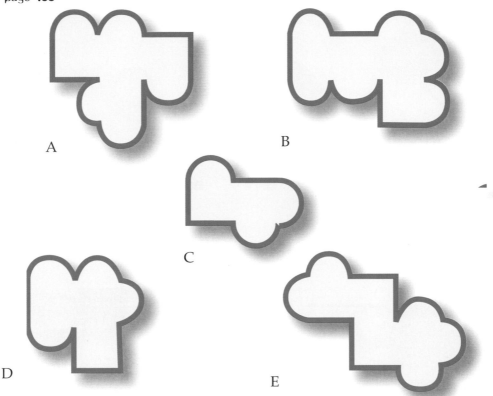

A

B

C

D

E

PUZZLE 156

These cars are all racing at famous circuits. Can you work out the number of the car at Indianapolis?

Answer see page **165**

No. 139

Silverstone

No. 101

Monaco

No. 98

Le Mans

No. 154

Monte Carlo

No. ?

Indianapolis

PUZZLE 157

Answer see page **165**

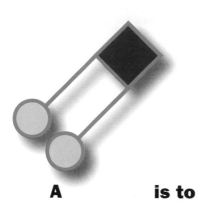 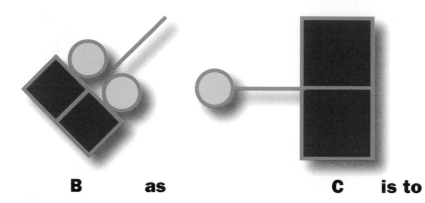

A   is to   **B**   as   **C**   is to

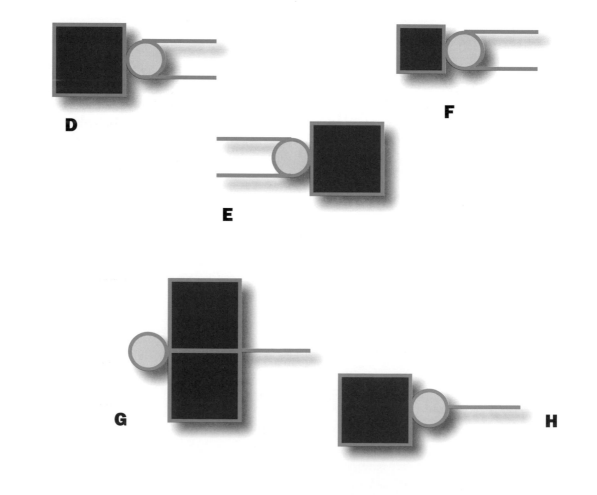

D

F

E

G

H

PUZZLE 158

Which of the following layouts could be used to make the above cube?

Answer see page **165**

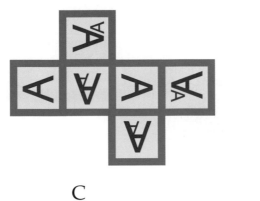

A

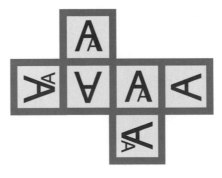

B

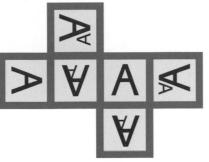

C

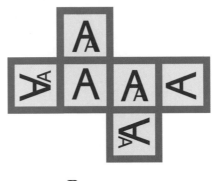

D

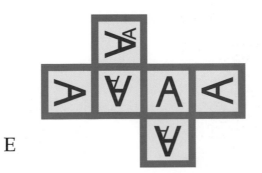

E

PUZZLE 159

Can you work out the logic behind this square and fill in the missing section?

Answer see page **165**

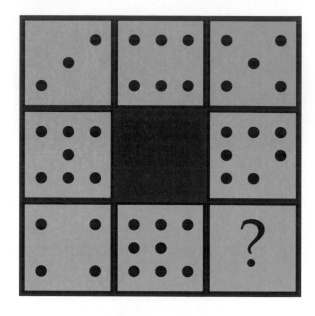

PUZZLE 160

The licence plates of all these cars conform to a certain logic. Can you work out the final plate?

Answer see page **165**

AEC 759

BFD 8610

GKI 1311

JNL 1614

Q ?

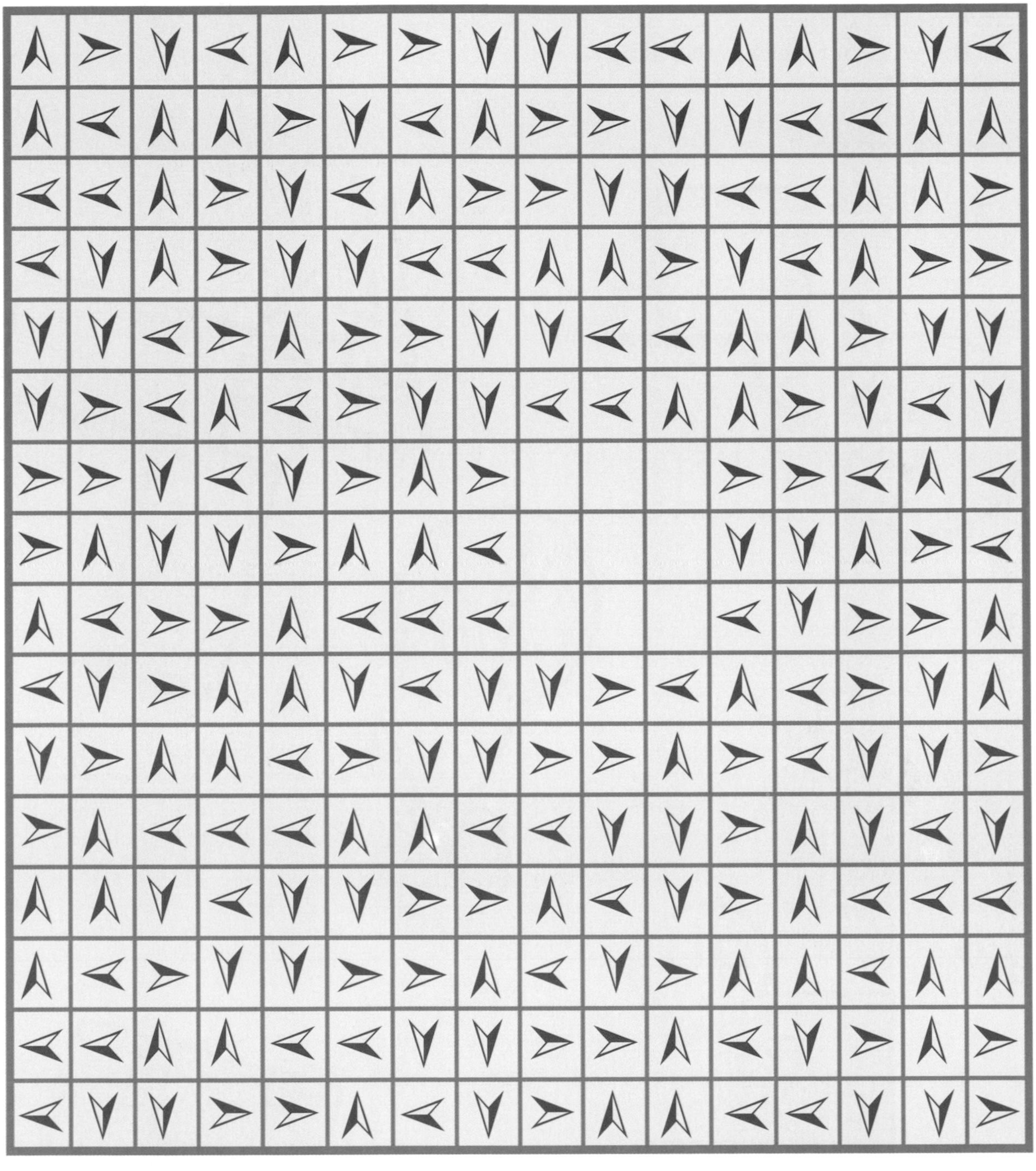

PUZZLE 161

Can you work out the reasoning behind this grid and complete the missing section?

Answer see page **165**

PUZZLE 162

Can you work out which is the odd
diagram out?

Answer see page **165**

PUZZLE 163

Can you work out which of these symbols comes next in this sequence?

Answer see page **165**

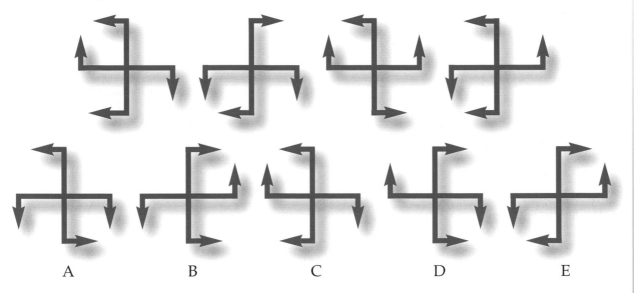

A   B   C   D   E

PUZZLE 164

Each balloon has been sponsored by a famous newspaper. The number is somehow linked to the paper's name. What is the number of *The Independent's* balloon?

Answer see page **165**

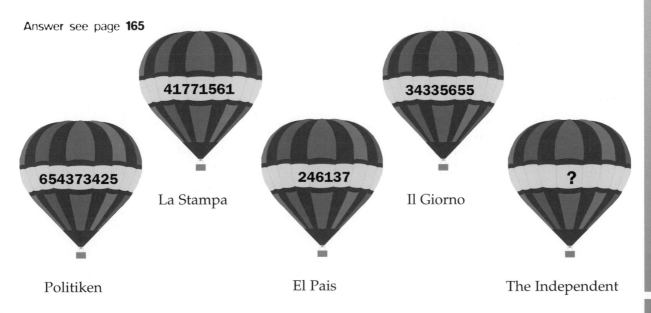

41771561 — La Stampa

654373425 — Politiken

246137 — El Pais

34335655 — Il Giorno

? — The Independent

PUZZLE 165

Can you work out the logic behind this square and find the missing number?

Answer see page **165**

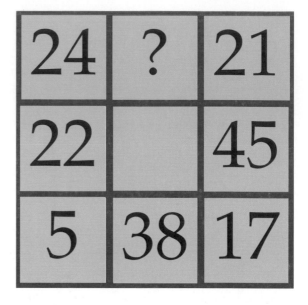

PUZZLE 166

Can you work out which symbol is the odd one out?

Answer see page **165**

A   B   C   D   E

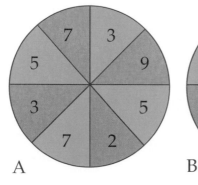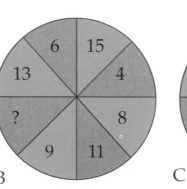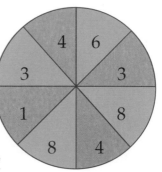

A   B   C

PUZZLE 167

Can you replace the question mark with a number?

Answer see page **165**

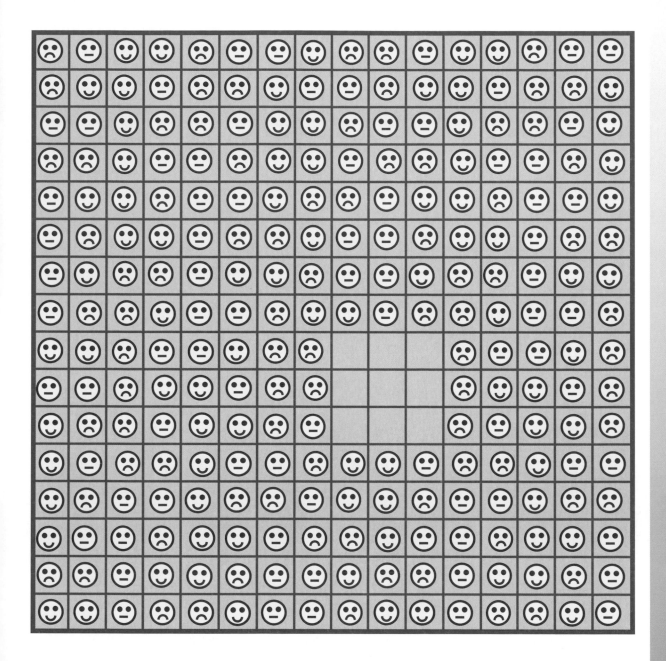

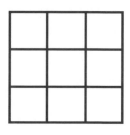

PUZZLE 168

This grid is made up according to a certain pattern. Can you work it out and fill in the missing section?

Answer see page **165**

PUZZLE 169

If you know that the answer forms a well-known sequence, can you work out how much each shape is worth?

Answer see page 165

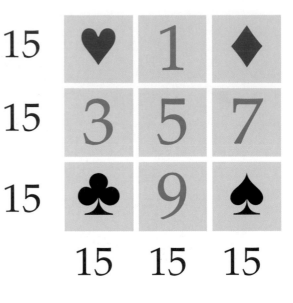

PUZZLE 170

Can you work out what the next matchstick man in this series should look like?

Answer see page 166

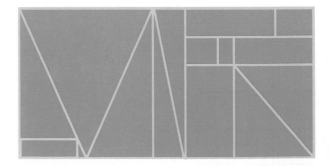

PUZZLE 171

Can you work out how many rectangles can be found in this diagram altogether?

Answer see page 166

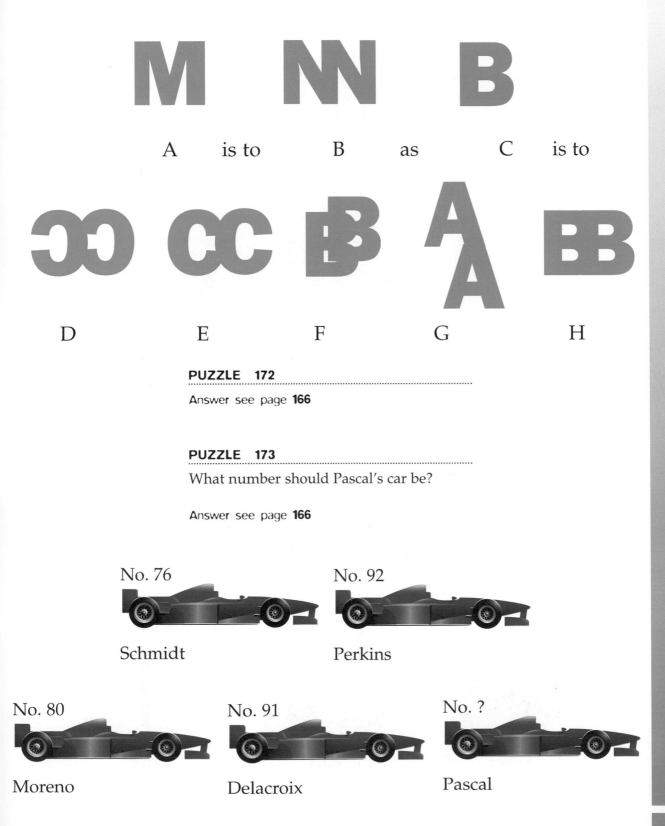

A   is to   B   as   C   is to

D   E   F   G   H

PUZZLE 172
....
Answer see page **166**

PUZZLE 173
....
What number should Pascal's car be?

Answer see page **166**

No. 76

Schmidt

No. 92

Perkins

No. 80

Moreno

No. 91

Delacroix

No. ?

Pascal

PUZZLE 174

Can you work out which of these cubes
cannot be made from the layout below?

Answer see page **166**

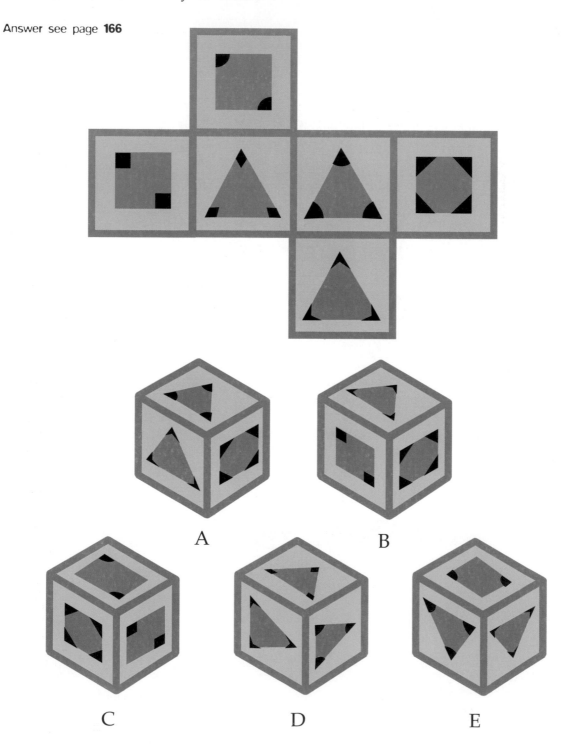

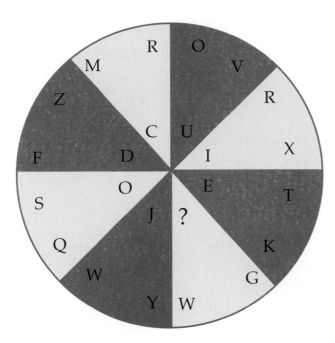

PUZZLE 175

Can you replace the question mark with a letter?

Answer see page **166**

PUZZLE 176

Can you work out which shape is the odd one out?

Answer see page **166**

A

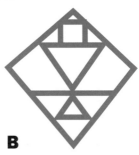

B

C

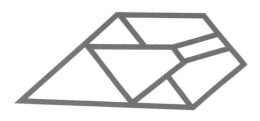

D

E

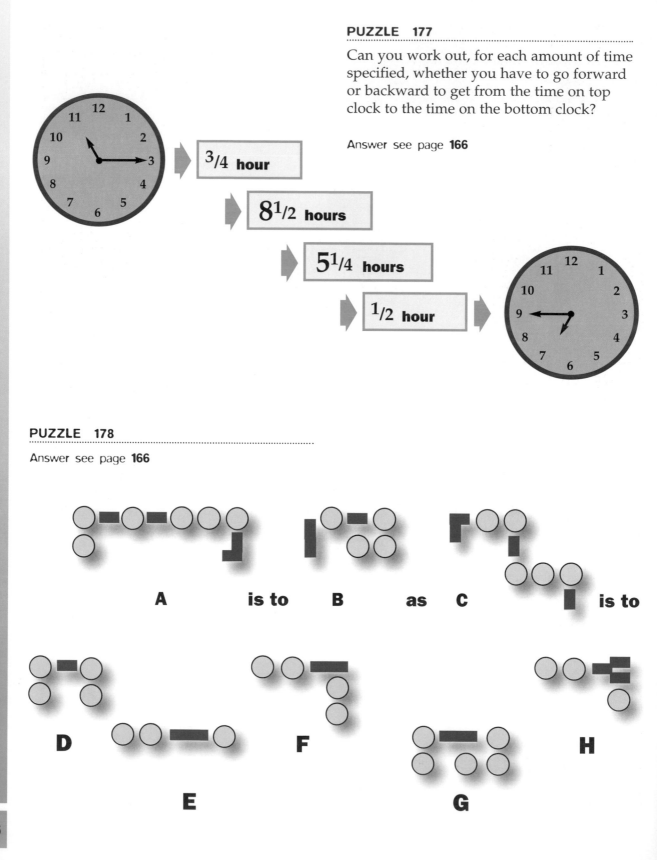

PUZZLE 177

Can you work out, for each amount of time specified, whether you have to go forward or backward to get from the time on top clock to the time on the bottom clock?

Answer see page **166**

3/4 hour

8¹/₂ hours

5¹/₄ hours

¹/₂ hour

PUZZLE 178

Answer see page **166**

A   **is to**   **B**   **as**   **C**   **is to**

D   **F**   **H**

E   **G**

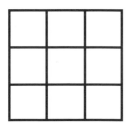

PUZZLE 179

Can you work out what pattern this grid follows and complete the missing section?

Answer see page **166**

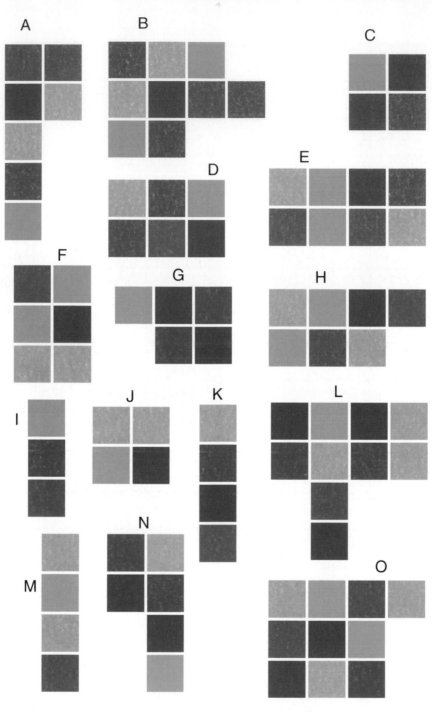

PUZZLE 180

The pieces given will, if put together correctly, make a square. One piece is not needed. Which of the given pieces is it?

Answer see page **166**

PUZZLE 181

Find the missing letter.

Answer see page 166

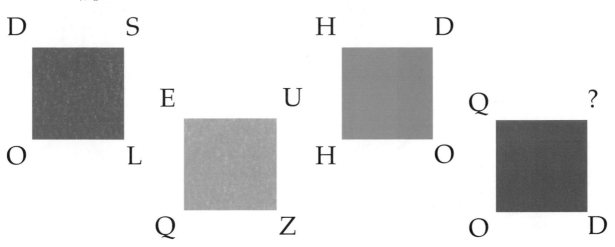

PUZZLE 182

Find the missing number.

Answer see page 166

PUZZLE 183

Find a number that could replace the question mark. Each color represents a number under 10.

Answer see page 166

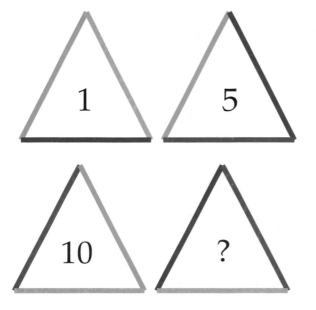

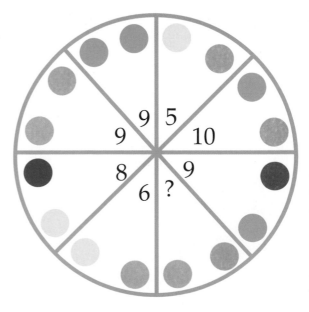

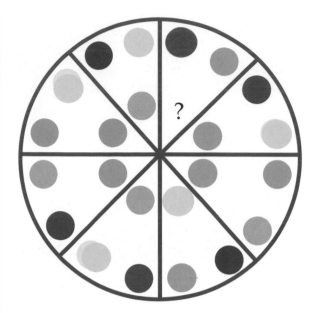

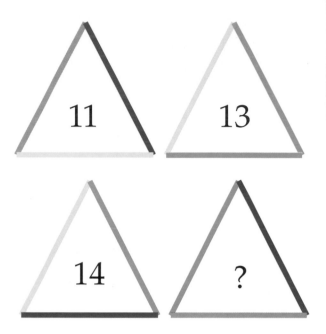

PUZZLE 184

Which color is the circle that replaces the question mark?

Answer see page **166**

PUZZLE 185

Find a number that could replace the question mark. Each color represents a number under 10.

Answer see page **166**

PUZZLE 186

Find the missing letter.
Answer see page **167**

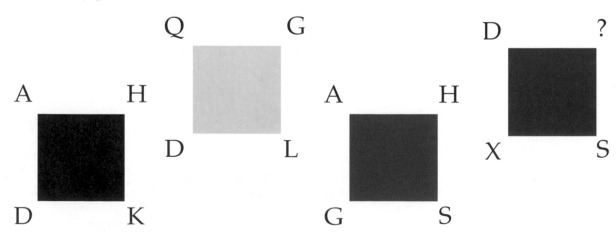

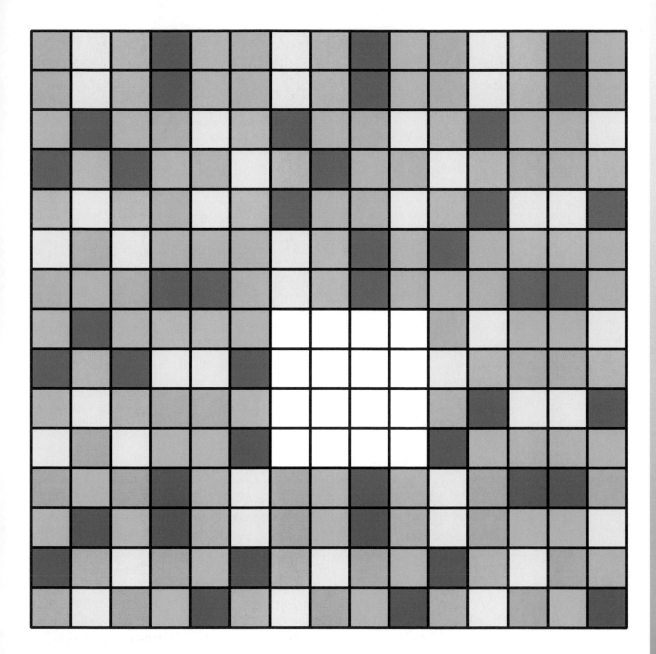

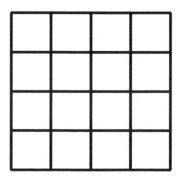

PUZZLE 187

This square is drawn according to a certain logic. If you can work out what the system is you should be able to fill in the missing area.

Answer see page **167**

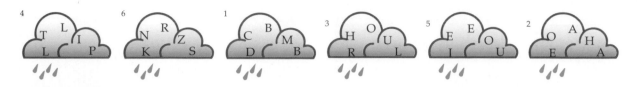

PUZZLE 188

Pick one letter from each cloud in order. You should be able to make the names of five composers.

Answer see page **167**

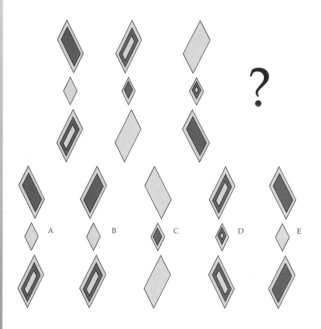

PUZZLE 189

Can you find the column that comes next in the sequence?

Answer see page **167**

PUZZLE 190

Can you work out what the next fish in this sequence should look like?

Answer see page **167**

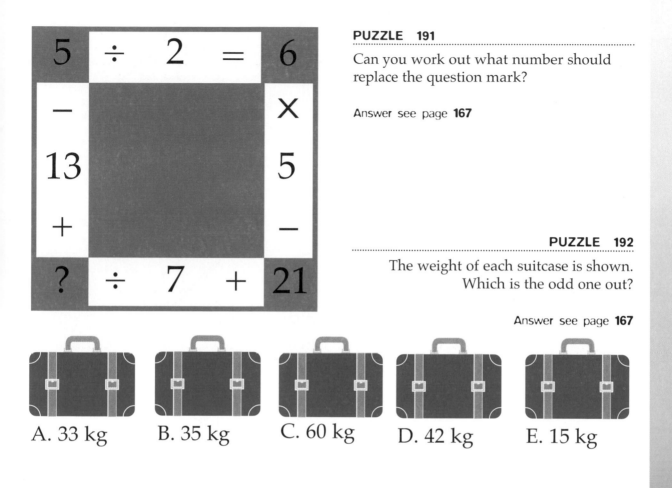

PUZZLE 191

Can you work out what number should replace the question mark?

Answer see page **167**

PUZZLE 192

The weight of each suitcase is shown. Which is the odd one out?

Answer see page **167**

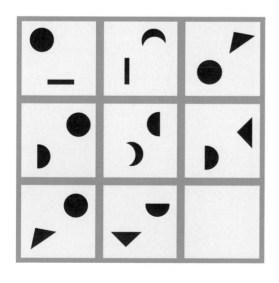

A. 33 kg   B. 35 kg   C. 60 kg   D. 42 kg   E. 15 kg

PUZZLE 193

Can you work out which of these squares would complete the above diagram?

Answer see page **167**

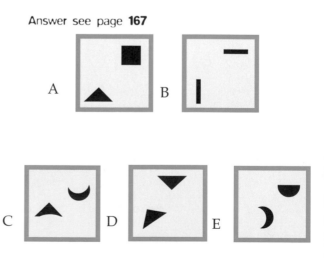

A   B   C   D   E

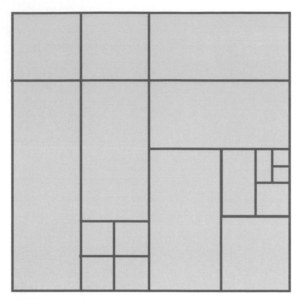

PUZZLE 194

How many squares can you find in this diagram altogether?

Answer see page **167**

PUZZLE 195

In this diagram the four basic mathematical signs (+, −, ×, ÷) have been left out. Can you replace the question marks?

Answer see page **167**

PUZZLE 196

Can you work out which of these shapes would fit together with the shape to the right?

Answer see page **167**

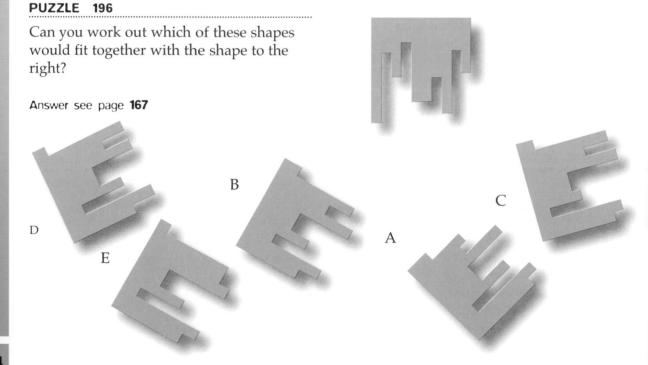

12   19

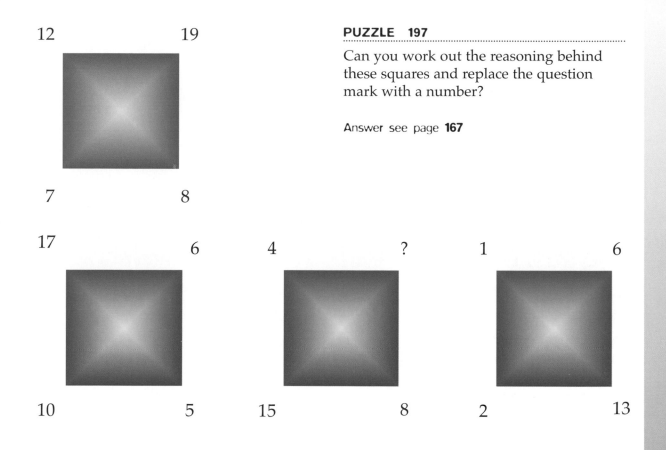

7   8

PUZZLE 197

Can you work out the reasoning behind these squares and replace the question mark with a number?

Answer see page **167**

17   6   4   ?   1   6

10   5   15   8   2   13

PUZZLE 198

Can you spot the cube that cannot be made from the layout below?

Answer see page **167**

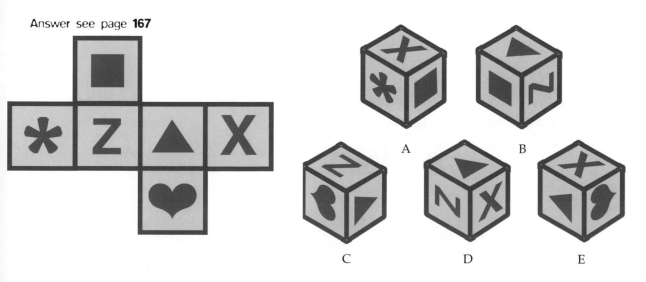

A   B

C   D   E

PUZZLE 199

Can you find the number that should replace the question mark?

Answer see page **167**

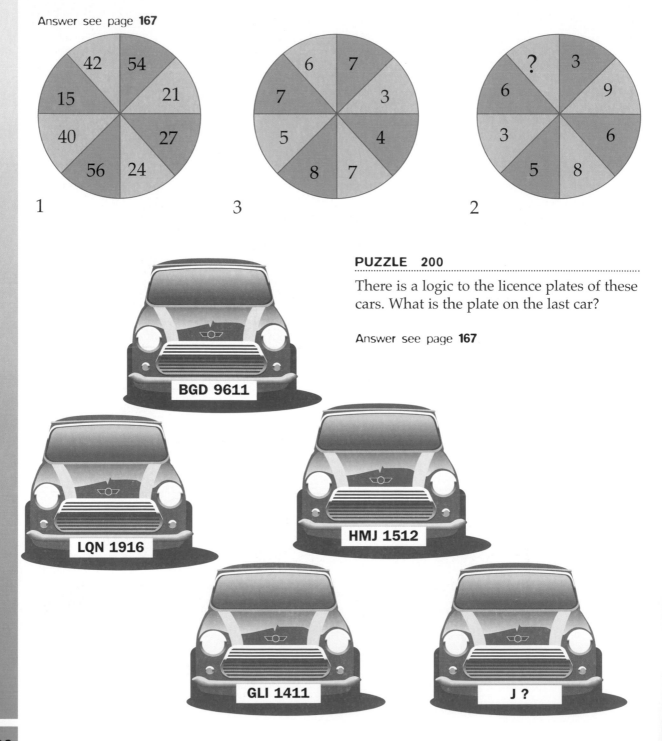

1

3

2

PUZZLE 200

There is a logic to the licence plates of these cars. What is the plate on the last car?

Answer see page **167**

BGD 9611

LQN 1916

HMJ 1512

GLI 1411

J ?

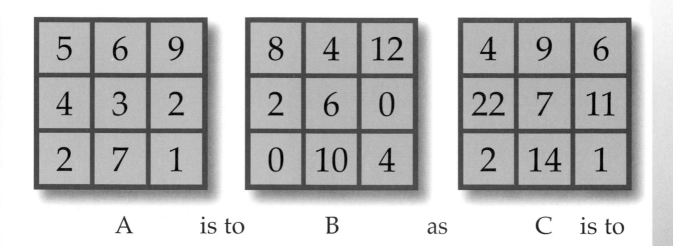

5	6	9
4	3	2
2	7	1

A   is to

8	4	12
2	6	0
0	10	4

B   as

4	9	6
22	7	11
2	14	1

C   is to

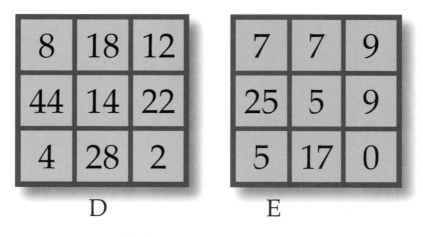

8	18	12
44	14	22
4	28	2

D

7	7	9
25	5	9
5	17	0

E

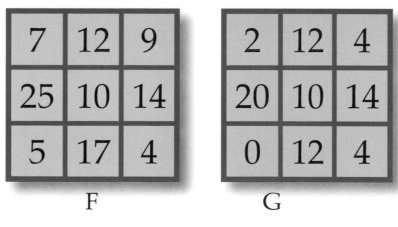

7	12	9
25	10	14
5	17	4

F

2	12	4
20	10	14
0	12	4

G

PUZZLE   201

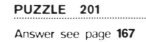

Answer see page **167**

127

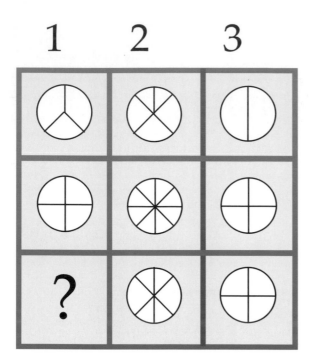

PUZZLE 202

Can you work out the reasoning behind this square and replace the question mark with the correct shape?

Answer see page **167**

PUZZLE 203

Can you find the letter that comes next in this series?

Answer see page **167**

PUZZLE 204

Take one letter from each bulb in order. You should be able to make five five-letter words related to food.

Answer see page **167**

PUZZLE 205

Can you work out which diagram would
continue the series?

Answer see page **168**

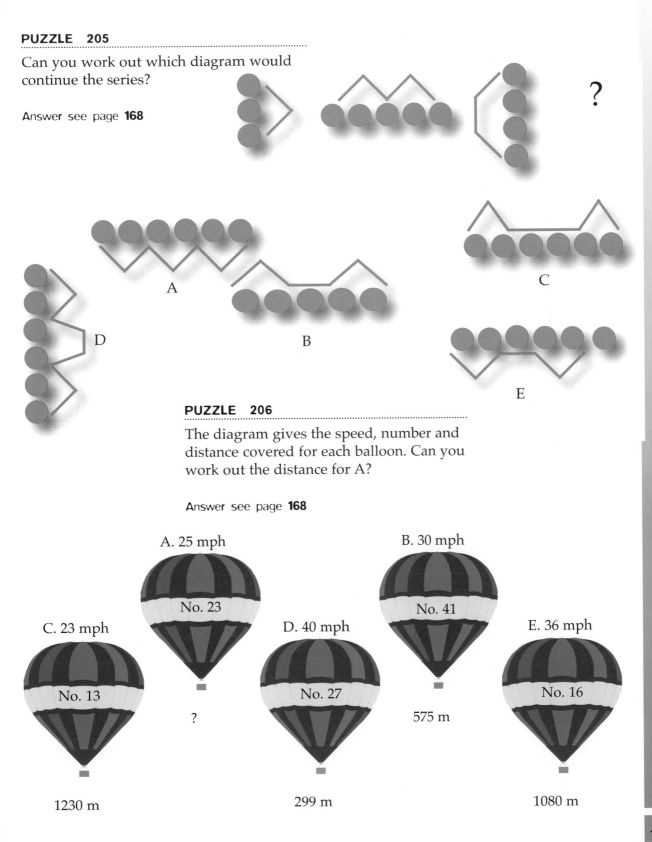

PUZZLE 206

The diagram gives the speed, number and
distance covered for each balloon. Can you
work out the distance for A?

Answer see page **168**

A. 25 mph
No. 23
?

B. 30 mph
No. 41
575 m

C. 23 mph
No. 13
1230 m

D. 40 mph
No. 27
299 m

E. 36 mph
No. 16
1080 m

PUZZLE 207

Can you work out which of these symbols
follows the sequence?

Answer see page **168**

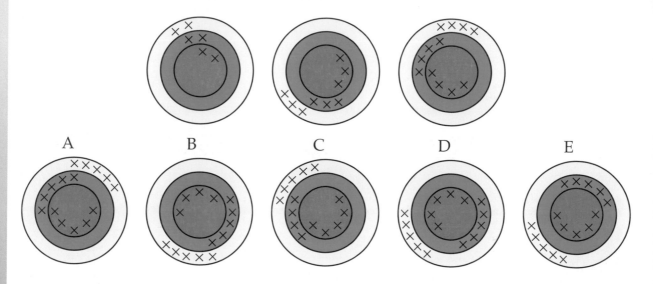

PUZZLE 208

Can you work out what number should
replace the question mark in this diagram?

Answer see page **168**

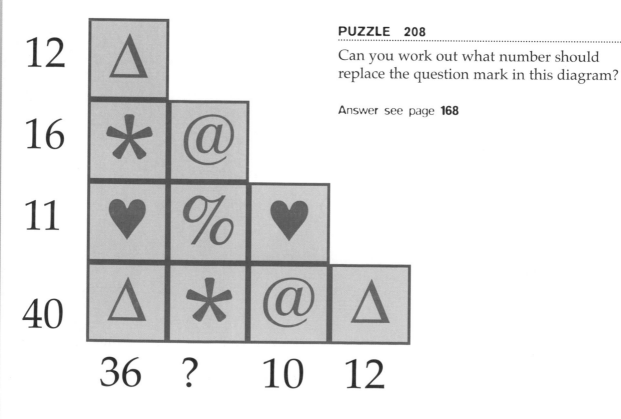

2	2	3	1	1	7	1	4	5	5	2	2	3	1	1	7
5	3	1	1	7	1	4	5	5	2	2	3	1	1	7	1
5	2	3	1	1	7	1	4	5	5	2	2	3	1	1	4
4	2	2	2	2	3	1	1	7	1	4	5	5	2	7	5
1	5	2	5	1	4	5	5	2	2	3	1	1	2	1	5
7	5	5	5	7	2	2	3	1	1	7	1	7	3	4	2
1	4	5	4	1	5	3	1	1	7	1	4	1	1	5	2
1	1	4	1	1	5	2	3	1	1	4	5	4	1	5	3
3	7	1	7	3	4	2	2	2	7	5	5	5	7	2	1
2	1	7	1	2	1	5	5	4	1	5	2	5	1	2	1
2	1	1	1	2	7	1	1	3	2	2	2	2	4	3	7
5	3	1	3	5	5	4	1	7	1	1	3	2	5	1	1
5	2	3	2	2	5	5	4	1	7	1	1	3	5	1	4
		2	5	5	4	1	7	1	1	3	2	2	7	5	
		4	1	7	1	1	3	2	2	5	5	4	1	5	
		3	2	2	5	5	4	1	7	1	1	3	2	2	

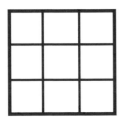

PUZZLE 209

Can you work out the reasoning behind this grid and complete the missing section?

Answer see page **168**

PUZZLE 210

Which of these cubes can be made from the above layout?

Answer see page **168**

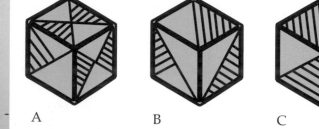  

A   B   C   D   E

PUZZLE 211

Can you work out which of these musical terms is the odd one out?

Answer see page **168**

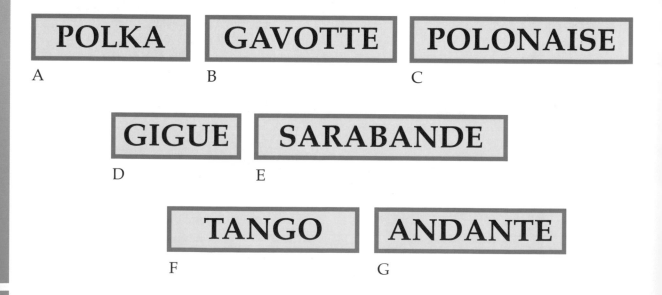

POLKA   GAVOTTE   POLONAISE
A   B   C

GIGUE   SARABANDE
D   E

TANGO   ANDANTE
F   G

PUZZLE 212

Can you work out the reasoning behind this wheel and replace the question mark with a number?

Answer see page 168

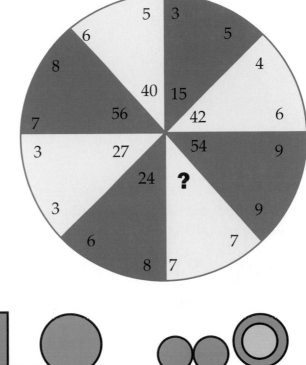

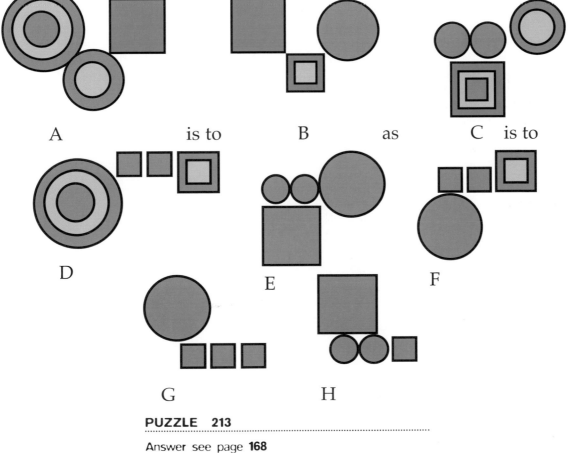

A   is to   B   as   C   is to

D   E   F

G   H

PUZZLE 213

Answer see page 168

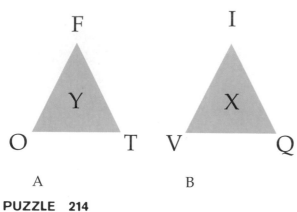

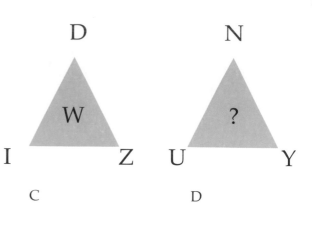

A　　　　**B**　　　　**C**　　　　**D**

PUZZLE 214

Can you work out what letter should replace the question mark?

Answer see page **168**

PUZZLE 215

Can you work out what the next grid in the sequence below should look like?

Answer see page **168**

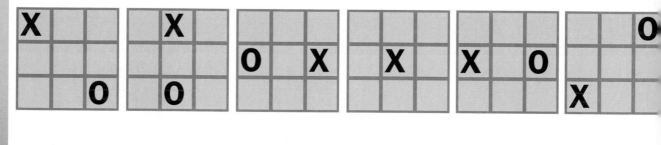

PUZZLE 216

Can you work out what the missing section in the last wheel should look like?

Answer see page **168**

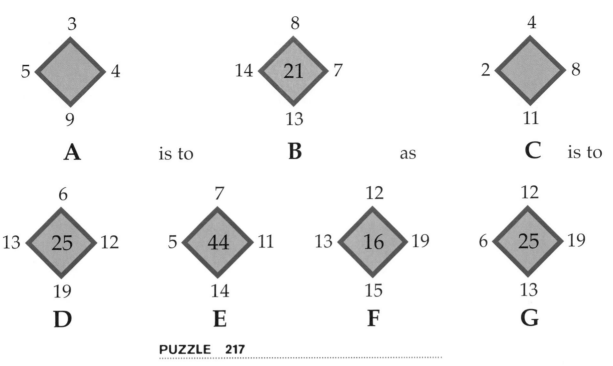

```
        3                          8                          4
   5  ◇  4                   14  ◇ 21 ◇ 7              2  ◇  8
        9                         13                         11

        A        is to           B          as            C     is to
```

```
        6                7                    12                   12
  13 ◇ 25 ◇ 12     5 ◇ 44 ◇ 11        13 ◇ 16 ◇ 19        6 ◇ 25 ◇ 19
       19               14                    15                   13

        D                E                     F                    G
```

PUZZLE 217

Answer see page **168**

PUZZLE 218

Can you find the letter that completes
this diagram?

Answer see page **168**

PUZZLE 219

Each horse carries a weight handicap.
Can you work out the number of the
final horse?

Answer see page **169**

B	P	?	F
D	N	T	D
F	L	V	B
H	J	X	Z

No. 4 15kg   No. 7 18kg   No. 3 14kg   No. 8 19kg   No. ? 24kg

135

1	2	2	3	4	4	1	2	3	3	4	1	2	2	3	4
3	3	2	1	4	4	3	2	2	1	4	3	3	2	1	4
4	1	2	2	3	4	4	1	2	3	3	4	1	2	2	3
3	2	1	4	4	3	2	2	1	4	3	3	2	1	4	4
3	4	1	2	2	3	4	4	1	2	3	3	4	1	2	2
2	1	4	4	3	2	2	1	4	3	3	2	1	4	4	3
3	3	4	1	2	2	3	4	4	1	2	3	3	4	1	2
1	4	4	3	2	2	1	4	3	3	2	1	4	4	3	2
2	3	3	4	1	2	2	3	4	4	1	2	3	3	4	1
4	4	3	2	2	1	4				1	4	4	3	2	2
1	2	3	3	4	1	2				4	1	2	3	3	4
4	3	2	2	1	4	3				4	4	3	2	2	1
4	1	2	3	3	4	1	2	2	3	4	4	1	2	3	3
3	2	2	1	4	3	3	2	1	4	4	3	2	2	1	4
4	4	1	2	3	3	4	1	2	2	3	4	4	1	2	3
2	2	1	4	3	3	2	1	4	4	3	2	2	1	4	3

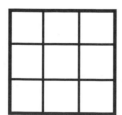

PUZZLE 220

Can you work out the reasoning behind this grid and complete the missing section?

Answer see page **169**

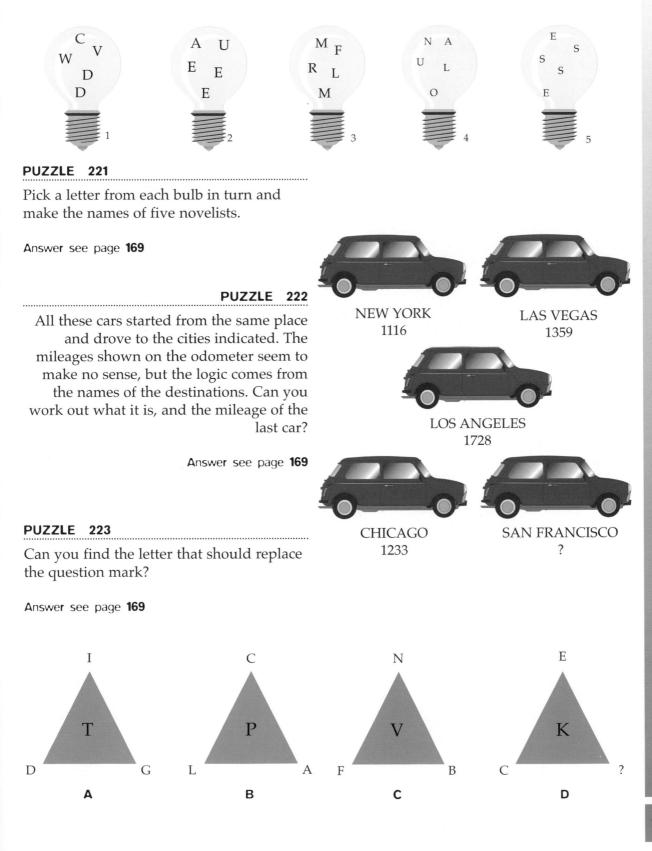

PUZZLE 221

Pick a letter from each bulb in turn and make the names of five novelists.

Answer see page **169**

PUZZLE 222

All these cars started from the same place and drove to the cities indicated. The mileages shown on the odometer seem to make no sense, but the logic comes from the names of the destinations. Can you work out what it is, and the mileage of the last car?

Answer see page **169**

NEW YORK
1116

LAS VEGAS
1359

LOS ANGELES
1728

CHICAGO
1233

SAN FRANCISCO
?

PUZZLE 223

Can you find the letter that should replace the question mark?

Answer see page **169**

A

B

C

D

PUZZLE 224

Can you work out which of these cubes cannot be made from the this layout?

Answer see page **169**

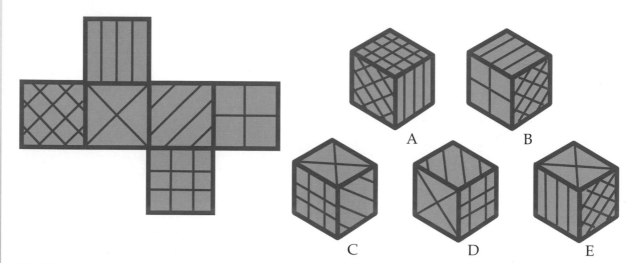

A   B

C   D   E

PUZZLE 225

Can you find the shape that would continue the series above?

Answer see page **169**

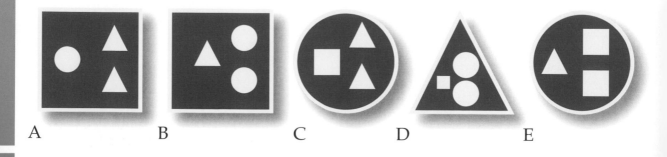

A   B   C   D   E

PUZZLE 226

Take one letter from each cloud in order. You should be able to make the names of five scientists.

Answer see page **169**

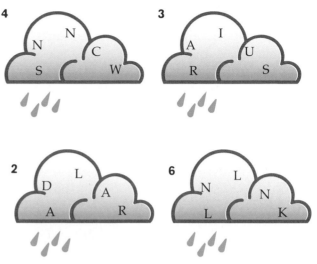

PUZZLE 227

Can you work out what letter should replace the question mark in this square?

Answer see page **169**

PUZZLE 228

All these bikes took part in an overnight race. Something really weird happened! The start and finish times of the bikes became mathematically linked. If you can discover the link you should be able to decide when bike D finished.

Answer see page **169**

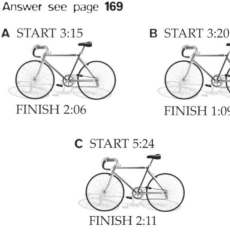

A START 3:15

FINISH 2:06

B START 3:20

FINISH 1:09

C START 5:24

FINISH 2:11

D START 7:35

FINISH ?

E START 6:28

FINISH 4:22

139

PUZZLE 229

Can you work out the reasoning behind
these squares and find the
missing number?

Answer see page **169**

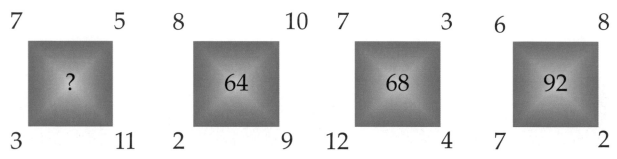

7   5   8   10   7   3   6   8

?   64   68   92

3   11   2   9   12   4   7   2

PUZZLE 230

To which of these diagrams could you add
a circle to match the conditions of the
figure at right?

Answer see page **169**

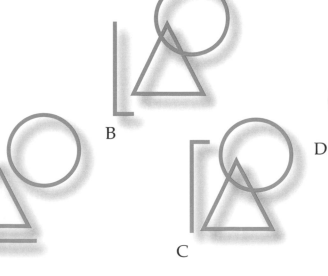

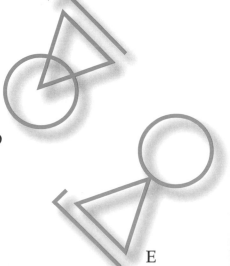

A

B

C

D

E

PUZZLE 231

Which of these shapes fits to complete the polygon?

Answer see page **169**

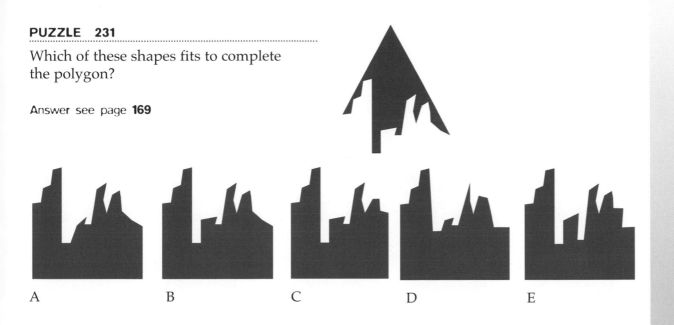

A   B   C   D   E

PUZZLE 232

All these horses are about to race at famous courses around the world. Which is the odd one out?

Answer see page **169**

A — BADEN-BADEN
B — EPSOM
C — LONGCHAMP
D — SARATOGA
E — NEWMARKET

PUZZLE 233

Can you replace the question mark with a number?

Answer see page **169**

4	× 3 +	8
=		÷
5		2
-		+
?	× 7 ÷	11

PUZZLE 234

Can you work out which of these squares
is the odd one out?

Answer see page **169**

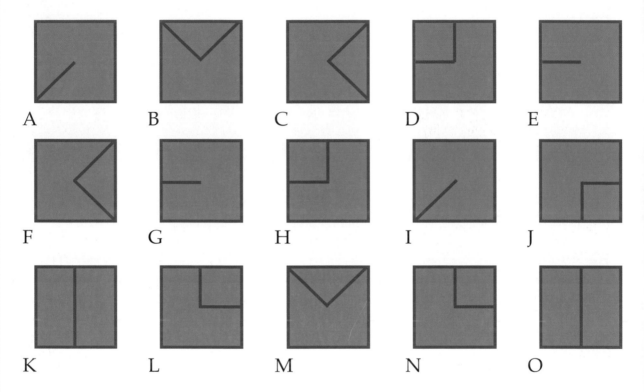

A   B   C   D   E

F   G   H   I   J

K   L   M   N   O

PUZZLE 235

Can you find the odd shape out?

Answer see page **169**

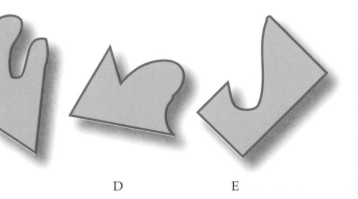

A   B   C   D   E

&	&	%	*	%	@	@	%	*	&	&	%	*	%	@	@
*	@	@	%	*	&	&	%	*	%	@	@	%	*	&	&
%	%	&	&	%	*	%	@	@	%	*	&	&	%	*	%
@	*	*	*	%	@	@	%	*	&	&	%	*	%	%	*
@	%	%	%	@				&	&	%	*	%	@	@	%
%	&	@	&	%				&	&	%	*	@	@	@	@
*	&	@	&	*				*	&	&	%	@	%	%	@
%	*	%	*	%	%	@	@	@	%	%	@	%	*	*	%
&	%	*	%	&	*	%	%	*	*	*	@	*	&	&	*
&	@	%	@	&	%	*	%	&	&	%	%	&	&	&	&
*	@	&	@	*	&	&	*	%	@	@	*	&	%	%	&
%	%	&	%	%	@	@	%	*	%	&	&	%	*	*	%
@	*	*	*	%	&	&	*	%	@	@	%	*	%	%	*
@	%	%	@	@	%	*	%	&	&	*	%	@	@	@	%
%	&	&	*	%	@	@	%	*	%	&	&	*	%	@	@
*	%	&	&	*	%	@	@	%	*	%	&	&	*	%	@

PUZZLE 236

Can you work out the pattern sequence and fill in the missing section?

Answer see page **169**

PUZZLE 237

Can you work out what number should replace the question mark?

Answer see page 169

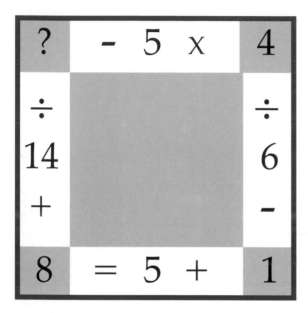

PUZZLE 239

Which cube can be made from this layout?

Answer see page 170

PUZZLE 238

Each farmer gets a different tonnage per acre. Somehow the number of tons is related to the letters in his name. How many tons does Grimble get? You need to find two possible values for each letter.

Answer see page 170

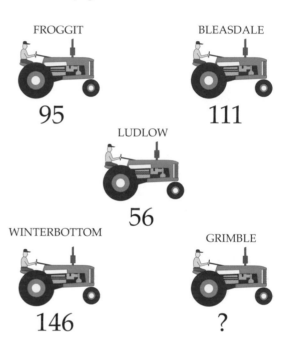

FROGGIT 95

BLEASDALE 111

LUDLOW 56

WINTERBOTTOM 146

GRIMBLE ?

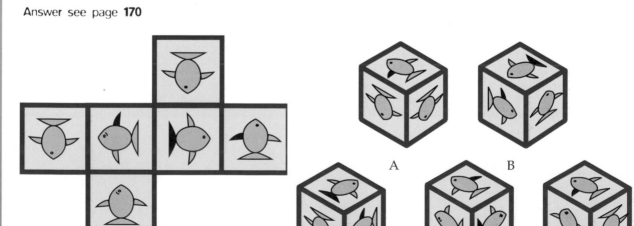

A   B

C   D   E

PUZZLE 240

Here is another diagam in which we have supplied the letters you do NOT need to complete the puzzle! When you have decided what letters are missing, rearrange them and you will find a city named after a US President.
Beware! One letter is used twice.

Answer see page **170**

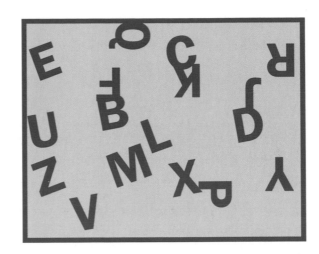

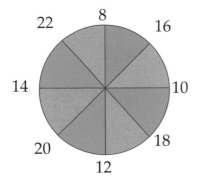

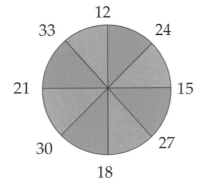

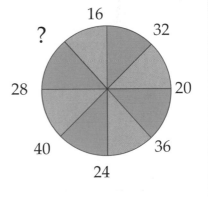

PUZZLE 241

Can you work out what number should replace the question mark?

Answer see page **170**

PUZZLE 242

Can you work out the reasoning behind these squares and find the number that should replace the question mark?

Answer see page **170**

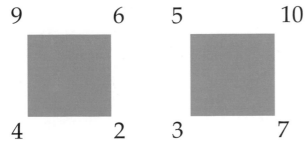

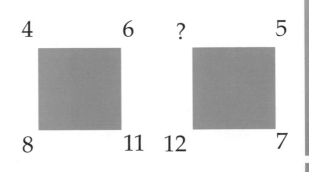

145

PUZZLE 243

Can you find the odd shape out?

Answer see page **170**

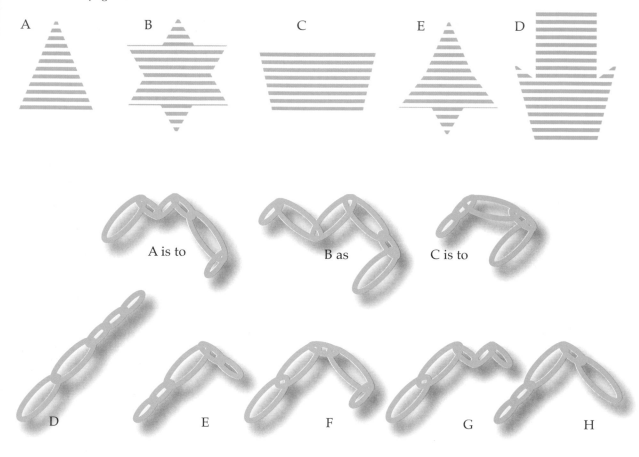

A   B   C   E   D

A is to   B as   C is to

D   E   F   G   H

PUZZLE 245

Answer see page **170**

PUZZLE 244

Pick one letter from each bulb in order.
You can make the names of five artists.

Answer see page **170**

M K
B M   1
B

A
L O   2
O
A

N
C I   3
N
S

C E
M E   4
O

N H
T T   5
T

PUZZLE 246

Can you find the odd diagram out?

Answer see page **170**

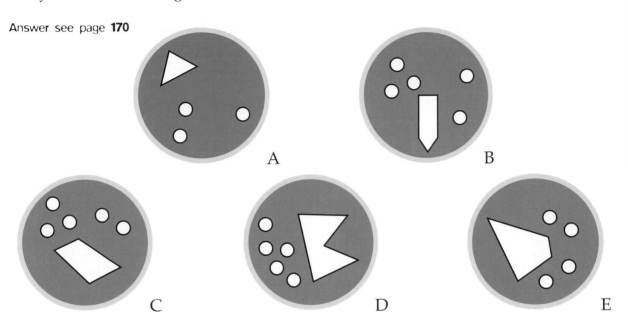

A

B

C

D

E

PUZZLE 247

Can you work out the reasoning behind this square and replace the question mark with a number?

Answer see page **170**

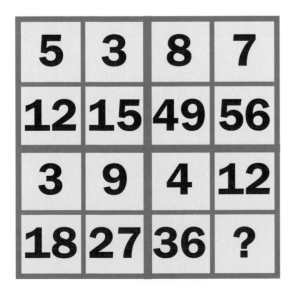

PUZZLE 248

The first interplanetary travellers are about to set off. Whose luggage is going to be put off at the wrong stop?

Answer see page **170**

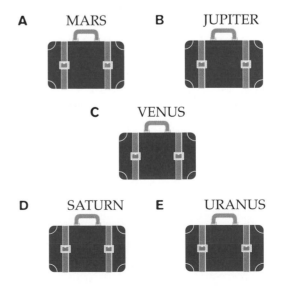

A   MARS   B   JUPITER

C   VENUS

D   SATURN   E   URANUS

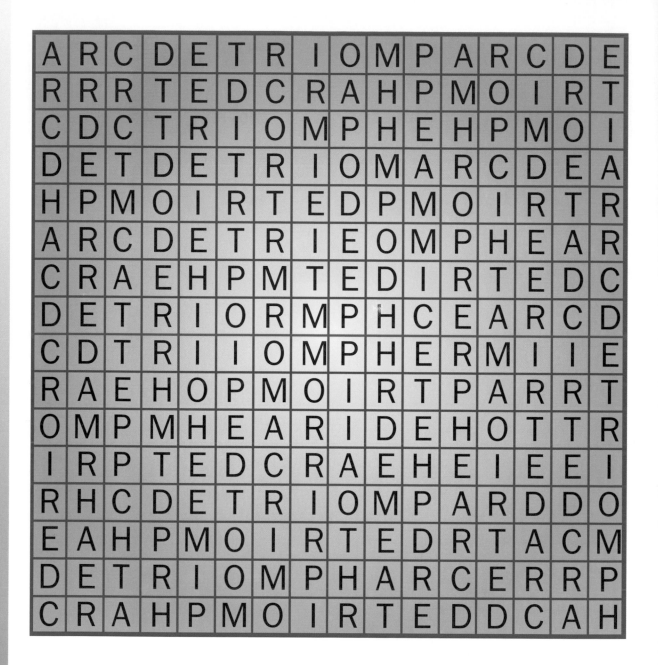

A	R	C	D	E	T	R	I	O	M	P	A	R	C	D	E
R	R	R	T	E	D	C	R	A	H	P	M	O	I	R	T
C	D	C	T	R	I	O	M	P	H	E	H	P	M	O	I
D	E	T	D	E	T	R	I	O	M	A	R	C	D	E	A
H	P	M	O	I	R	T	E	D	P	M	O	I	R	T	R
A	R	C	D	E	T	R	I	E	O	M	P	H	E	A	R
C	R	A	E	H	P	M	T	E	D	I	R	T	E	D	C
D	E	T	R	I	O	R	M	P	H	C	E	A	R	C	D
C	D	T	R	I	I	O	M	P	H	E	R	M	I	I	E
R	A	E	H	O	P	M	O	I	R	T	P	A	R	R	T
O	M	P	M	H	E	A	R	I	D	E	H	O	T	T	R
I	R	P	T	E	D	C	R	A	E	H	E	I	E	E	I
R	H	C	D	E	T	R	I	O	M	P	A	R	D	D	O
E	A	H	P	M	O	I	R	T	E	D	R	T	A	C	M
D	E	T	R	I	O	M	P	H	A	R	C	E	R	R	P
C	R	A	H	P	M	O	I	R	T	E	D	D	C	A	H

PUZZLE 249

The phrase ARC DE TRIOMPHE is
concealed somewhere in this grid.
It occurs in its entirety only once. It is
written in straight lines with only one
change of direction. Can you find it?

Answer see page **170**

PUZZLE 250

Can you work out what the next wheel in this sequence should look like?

Answer see page **170**

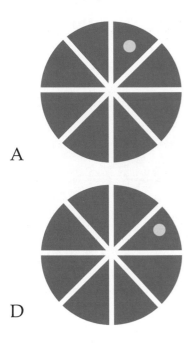

A

B

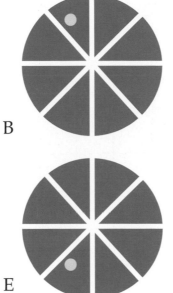

C

D

E

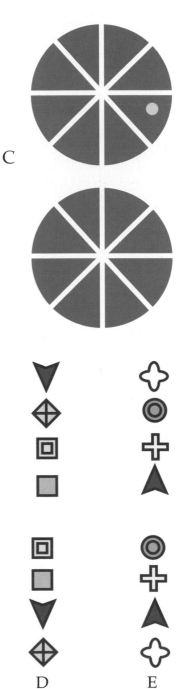

PUZZLE 251

Which of these columns would continue the sequence to the right?

Answer see page **170**

A   B   C   D   E

PUZZLE 252

Can you work out which symbol is the odd one out?

Answer see page **170**

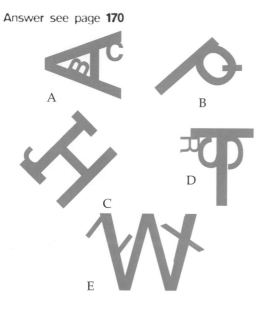

A
B
D
C
E

PUZZLE 253

All these horses are ready for the off. Which is the odd one out?

Answer see page **170**

SOLAR SPRINTER

SILVER STREAK

SLY SKY

SUPER SAVAGE   STEEL SABER

PUZZLE 254

Can you find the odd diagram out?

Answer see page **171**

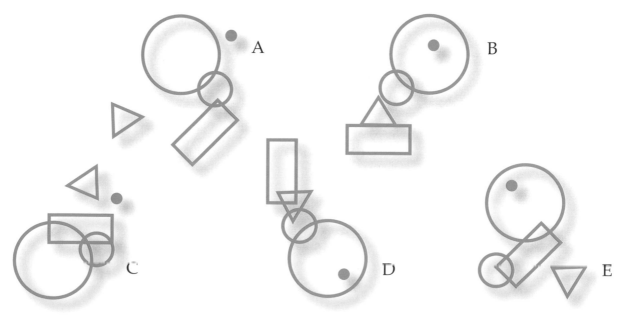

A
B
C
D
E

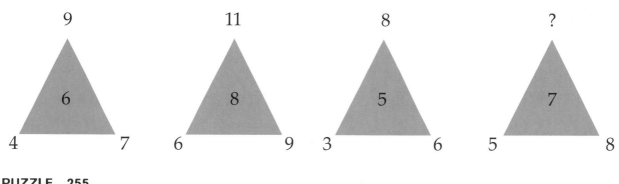

PUZZLE 255

Can you work out the logic behind these triangles and replace the question mark with a number?

Answer see page **171**

PUZZLE 256

Can you work out what number should replace the question mark?

Answer see page **171**

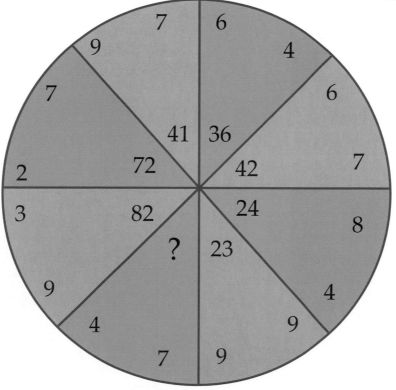

PUZZLE 257

Can you work out which of these diagrams
would continue the series?

Answer see page 171

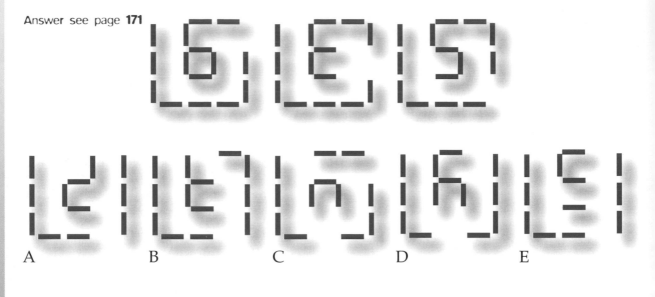

A   B   C   D   E

PUZZLE 258

Which of these shapes should replace the
question mark?

Answer see page 171

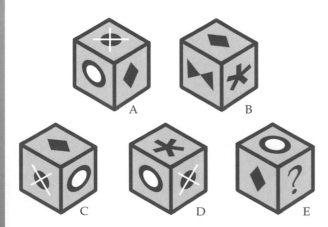

PUZZLE 259

Can you unravel the logic behind this
square and find the missing letter?

Answer see page 171

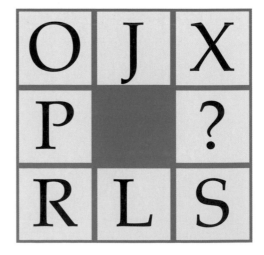

PUZZLE 260

The number of each train and its destination are in some way related. Can you work out where train No. 428 is bound for?

Answer see page **171**

No. 220
Denver

No. 47
Kansas City

No. 25
Galveston

No. 363
Lafayette

No. 428

a) Portland
b) Chicago
c) Nashville
d) Buffalo

PUZZLE 261

Take one letter from each of these bulbs in order. You will be able to make the names of five poets.

Answer see page **171**

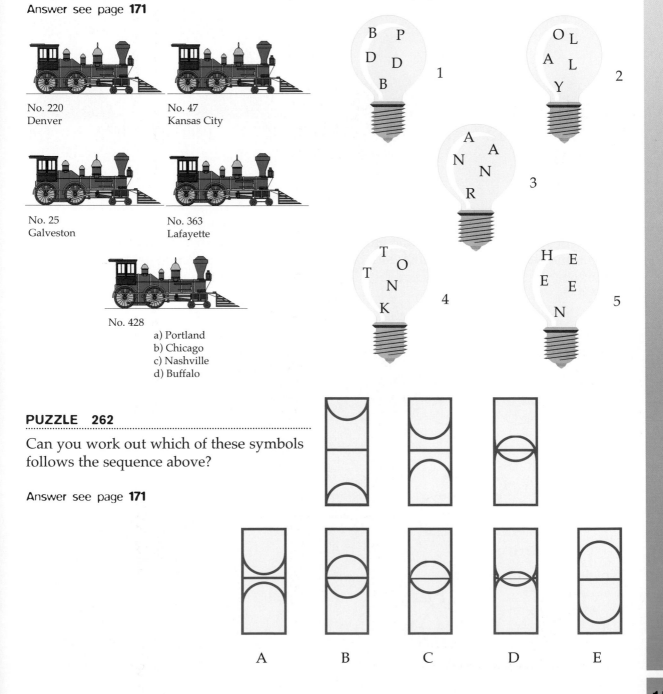

PUZZLE 262

Can you work out which of these symbols follows the sequence above?

Answer see page **171**

A   B   C   D   E

PUZZLE 263

Can you work out the reasoning behind these triangles and replace the question mark with a number?

Answer see page **171**

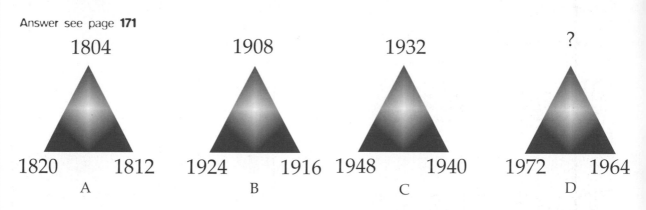

1804

1820   1812

A

1908

1924   1916

B

1932

1948   1940

C

?

1972   1964

D

PUZZLE 264

Five cyclists are taking part in a race. The number of each rider and its arrival time are in some way related. Can you work out the number of the rider who arrives at 2:30?

Answer see page **171**

PUZZLE 265

Using the amounts of time specified, can you work out whether you have to go forward or backward to get from the time on the top clock to that on the bottom clock?

Answer see page **171**

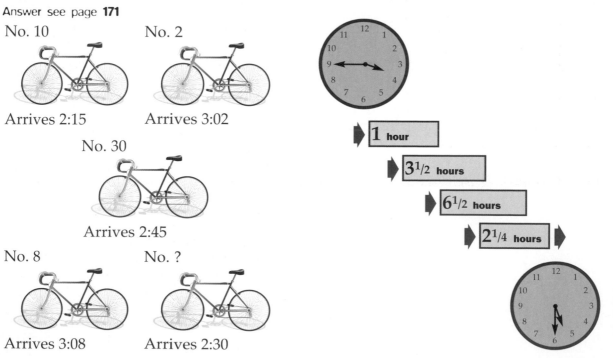

No. 10

Arrives 2:15

No. 2

Arrives 3:02

No. 30

Arrives 2:45

No. 8

Arrives 3:08

No. ?

Arrives 2:30

1 hour

31/2 hours

61/2 hours

21/4 hours

S	T	A	T	U	E	O	R	T	S	T	A	T	U	E	S
S	R	E	B	I	L	F	O	E	U	T	A	T	A	T	D
L	S	T	A	T	U	L	I	B	E	R	T	O	F	F	A
I	L	I	B	E	R	T	E	L	I	B	E	R	L	O	T
B	O	F	L	I	B	U	E	O	S	T	A	I	F	S	U
E	T	S	T	A	T	U	E	O	F	S	B	T	S	O	F
R	O	F	L	A	S	U	F	T	L	E	T	T	A	S	L
T	I	C	T	B	T	L	R	I	T	Y	A	S	T	T	I
Y	U	S	E	A	I	S	B	Y	T	T	A	T	U	A	B
E	L	I	T	B	B	E	E	S	T	A	T	U	E	T	E
R	T	S	E	Y	R	Y	T	R	E	B	L	F	O	U	R
S	T	R	A	T	U	S	O	F	L	I	B	E	R	T	Y
L	T	I	S	B	E	T	O	F	S	T	A	T	U	E	O
Y	T	A	T	U	E	A	F	O	T	R	E	B	I	L	F
E	B	I	L	F	O	T	S	T	A	T	U	E	O	E	L
R	T	S	T	A	T	U	T	S	F	O	T	R	E	B	I

PUZZLE 266

The phrase STATUE OF LIBERTY is concealed in this grid. It occurs only once in its entirety. Can you find it? It is written in straight lines with only one change of direction.

Answer see page **171**

PUZZLE 267

Can you work out what letter should replace the question mark in this square?

Answer see page **171**

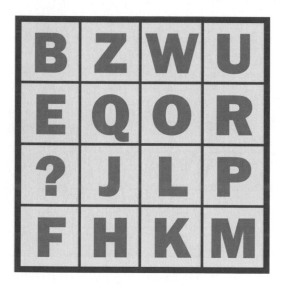

PUZZLE 268

The following clock faces are in some way related. Can you work out what the time on clock No. 3 should be?

Answer see page **171**

PUZZLE 269

Can you work out what number should replace the question mark in this square?

Answer see page **171**

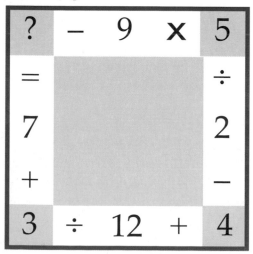

PUZZLE 270

Which diagram is the odd one out?

Answer see page **171**

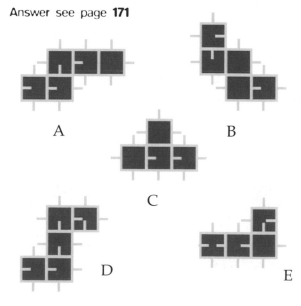

PUZZLE 271

Can you work out which of these cubes is not the same as the others?

Answer see page **171**

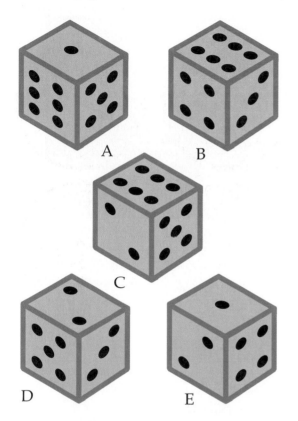

PUZZLE 272

Each tractor gathers potatoes over a certain acreage (shown in brackets). The weight of potatoes in kilos is shown under each tractor. There is a relationship between the number of the tractor, the acreage and the weight gathered. What weight should tractor B show?

Answer see page **171**

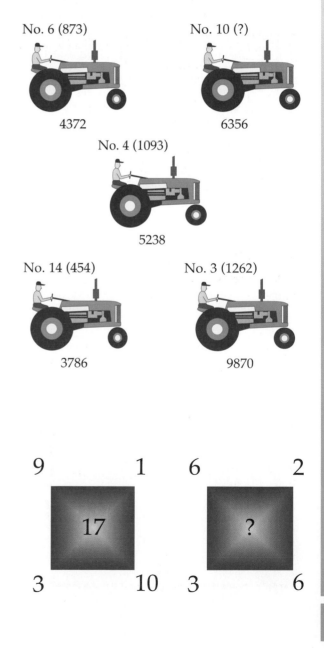

No. 6 (873)
4372

No. 10 (?)
6356

No. 4 (1093)
5238

No. 14 (454)
3786

No. 3 (1262)
9870

PUZZLE 273

Can you unravel the logic behind these squares and find the missing number?

Answer see page **172**

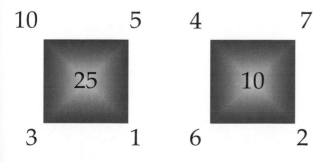

10		5
	25	
3		1

4		7
	10	
6		2

9		1
	17	
3		10

6		2
	?	
3		6

PUZZLE 274

Can you work out what the next flower in this series should look like?

Answer see page **172**

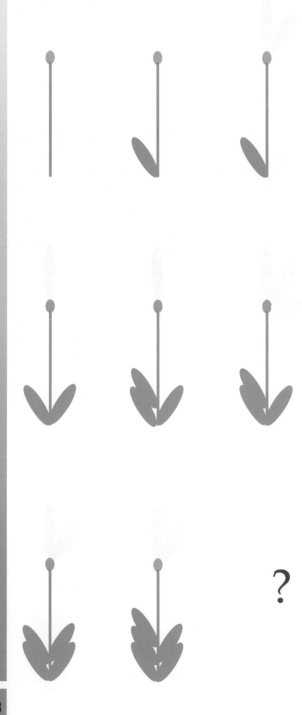

?

PUZZLE 275

Can you find the missing number in this square?

Answer see page **172**

1536	48	96	3
384	192	24	12
768	96	48	6
192	?	12	24

PUZZLE 276

Five cyclists are taking part in a race. The number of each rider and his cycling time are related to each other. Can you work out the number of the last cyclist?

Answer see page **172**

No. 9 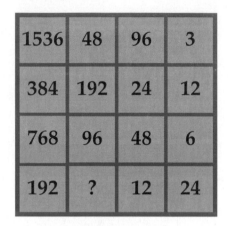 No. 10

Takes 1 hr 35   Takes 1 hr 43

No. 11

Takes 1 hr 52

No. 14 No. ?

Takes 2 hr 27   Takes 2 hr 33

S	E	R	E	P	E	N	S	T	I	N	E	R	E	S	E
E	E	S	E	N	R	P	E	N	S	E	R	P	E	N	T
R	S	R	S	E	I	S	R	T	E	R	P	E	N	T	I
P	E	P	P	S	E	T	P	I	N	E	N	E	S	S	S
E	R	E	S	N	T	N	N	N	E	R	I	N	N	N	E
N	P	N	E	R	T	E	T	E	P	N	S	E	E	I	R
T	E	T	R	P	S	I	I	T	P	T	P	T	R	T	P
N	N	I	P	E	E	N	N	T	R	R	S	E	P	N	E
E	T	N	E	N	T	E	E	E	E	S	E	T	E	E	N
I	N	E	N	T	R	S	E	S	R	E	T	S	N	P	T
S	E	R	T	P	E	N	T	I	N	E	T	S	T	R	I
S	E	R	N	P	E	N	T	I	N	E	E	N	I	E	T
E	S	R	E	I	S	E	R	P	E	N	T	I	N	S	E
S	E	T	E	N	N	I	T	N	E	P	R	E	S	T	E
R	S	E	N	E	I	T	N	I	P	R	E	S	E	S	T
S	E	R	P	E	N	S	N	I	T	N	E	P	R	E	S

PUZZLE 277

The word SERPENTINE is hidden somewhere in this grid. It occurs in its entirety only once. Can you find it? It may be spelled in any direction but is all in one line.

Answer see page **172**

PUZZLE 278

Find the missing number.

Answer see page **172**

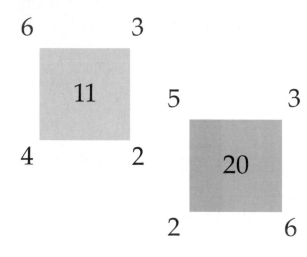
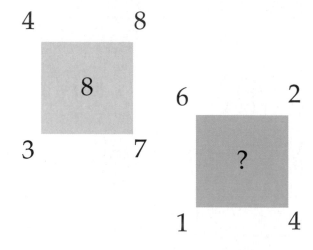

PUZZLE 279

Which of these triangles is the odd one out? Their color is a factor.

Answer see page **172**

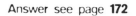

PUZZLE 280

Find a number that could replace the question mark. Each color represents a number under 10.

Answer see page **172**

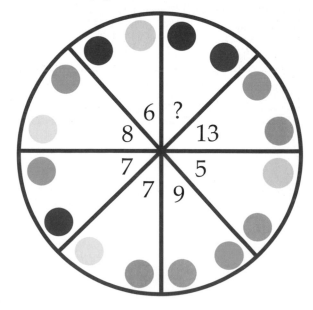

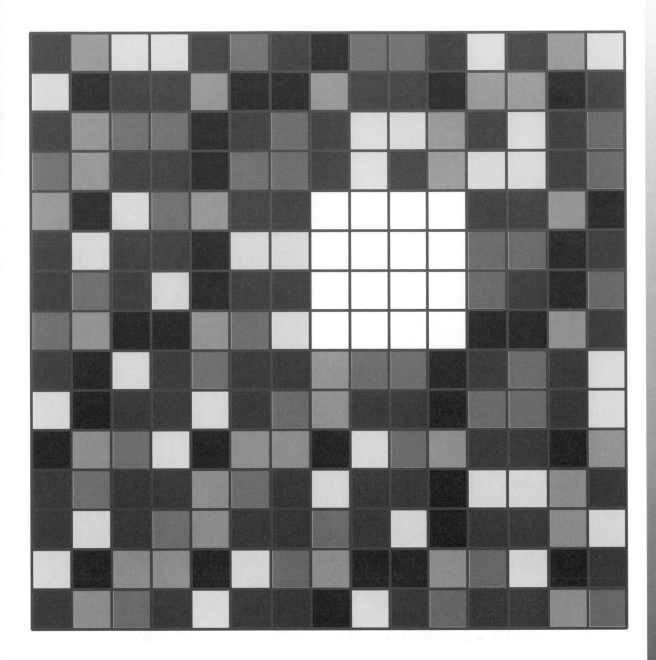

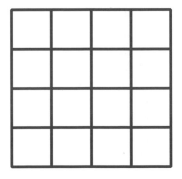

PUZZLE 281

The small squares form a logical sequence. If you can discover what that sequence is you should be able to complete the missing section.

Answer see page **172**

PUZZLE 282

Find a number that could replace the question mark. Each color represents a number under 10.

Answer see page **172**

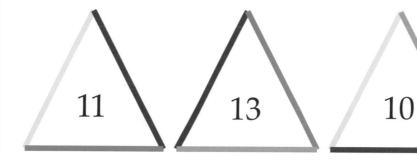

PUZZLE 283

Find a number that could replace the question mark. Each color represents a number under 10.

Answer see page **172**

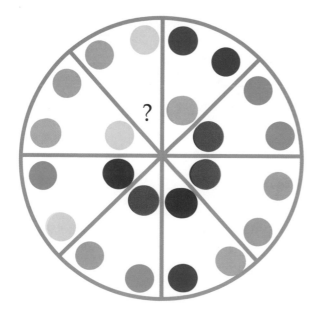

PUZZLE 284

Find a number that could replace the question mark. Each color represents a number under 10.

Answer see page **172**

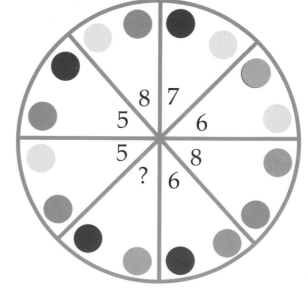

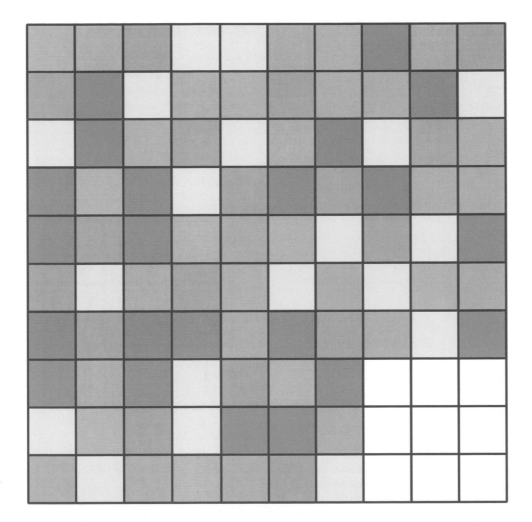

A

B

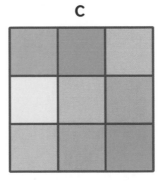

C

PUZZLE 285

Which of the sections shown would logically complete the puzzle?

Answer see page **172**

Answer 135
F. A curve turns into a straight line and a straight line into a curve.

Answer 136
C. It is the only one that does not have half as many 'step' lines as there are triangles.

Answer 137
B. It is the only figure that, with an additional line, has a triangle adjoining the rectangle that overlaps the square.

Answer 138
N. Going from the top to the bottom of one domino piece, then to the top of the next piece, etc., alternately move forward five letters and three back.

Answer 139
$- \times + - \div +.$ $9 - 3 \times 4 + 19 - 8 \div 5 + 4 = 11.$

Answer 140
D. All the others are cities, Kansas is a state (Kansas City actually straddles the Missouri-Kansas border).

Answer 141
Half circle. The shapes form two series that go from top to bottom of succeeding squares, and swap horizontally on the bottom squares. The sequence of shading is: quarter, half, three-quarters, fully shaded.

Answer 142
E. A square becomes a circle, a circle a triangle, and a triangle a square of similar proportions and positions.

Answer 143
Idaho, Iowa, Maine, Texas, Utah. The dummy letters are K and L.

Answer 144
C.

Answer 145
8. The sum of hands on each clock is 13.

Answer 146
I. It is based on the number alphabet backwards. Add the top and bottom rows together and put the sum in the middle.

Answer 147
The pattern sequence is:

Z R T T U W W Z Z S

Start at the bottom right and work up in a horizontal boustrophedon.

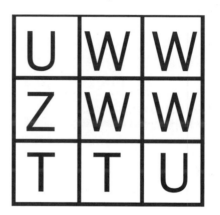

Answer 148
B. It is the only one with the same number of vertical and horizontal lines.

Answer 149
84. Multiply the hours of A by the minutes of B to get the tonnage of C, then B hours by C minutes to get D, C hours by D minutes to get E, D hours by E minutes to get A, and E hours by A minutes to get the tonnage of B.

Answer 150
G. The top and bottom elements swap position, the smaller central element becomes smaller still, and all three elements move inside the larger central shape.

Answer 151
E. Based on the position of the letters in the alphabet, multiply column 1 by column 3 and place the product in the middle column.

Answer 152
E.

Answer 153
B.

Answer 154
E. The shape has been folded along a horizontal line. A shaded piece covers an unshaded one.

Answer 155
B. The others all have an equal number of straight lines and curves.

Answer 156
No 201. Add together the values of the letters based on their reversed alphabetical position, (A = 26, Z = 1).

Answer 157
D. A circle becomes a square, a line a circle, and a square a line, all in the same size and position as original.

Answer 158
D.

Answer 159
It should have two dots. Add together the corner squares of each row or column and put the sum in the middle square of the opposite row or column.

Answer 160
QUS 2321. Go forward by 4 and back by 2 in the alphabet, then continue with numbers taken from the letters' alphabetical position.

Answer 161
The pattern sequence is as follows.

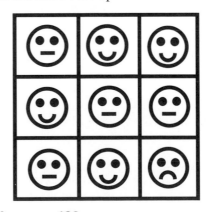

and spirals in a clockwise direction from the bottom left.

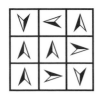

Answer 162
C. It is the only one to have an odd number of one element.

Answer 163
D. Alternate between rotating the pattern 90° counterclockwise, and swapping direction of each individual arrow.

Answer 164
72335226252257. The numbers are in code from the newspaper titles. A–C = 1, D–F = 2, G–I = 3, J–L = 4, M–O = 5, P–R = 6 S–U = 7, V–X = 8, Y–Z = 9.

Answer 165
29. Add together the corner squares of each row or column in a clockwise direction. Put the sum in the middle of the next row or column.

Answer 166
D. All the others are symmetrical.

Answer 167
12. Add together the values in the same segments in wheels A and C and put the answer in the opposite segment in wheel B.

Answer 168
The faces pattern sequence is smiley, smiley, straight, sad, sad, smiley, straight, straight, sad, etc. Start at the bottom left and work in a horizontal boustrophedon.

Answer 169
Spade = 2, Club = 4, Diamond = 6, Heart = 8.

Answer 170
The pattern is +1 lines, +2, +3, –2, –1, +1, +2, +3, etc. A figure with an even number of lines (ignoring the head) is turned upside down.

Answer 171
23.

Answer 172
E. Two letters following the first example, facing each other, run into each other

Answer 173
No. 52. Add together the value of the letters based on their alphabet position.

Answer 174
E.

Answer 175
B. Based on the number alphabet backwards, add the values of the two letters on the outer edge of each segment and place the sum into the opposite segment on the inside.

Answer 176
B. It consists of 14 straight lines, the rest of 13.

Answer 177
Back, back, forward, back.

Answer 178
F. Circles and rectangles interchange except for strings of 3 circles, which disappear.

Answer 179
The pattern sequence is: 1:00, 2:00, 2:00, 1:00, 3:00, 3:00, 2:00, 4:00, 4:00. 3:00, 5:00, 5:00, 4:00, 6:00, 6:00. Starting at the bottom left, work upwards in a vertical boustrophedon.

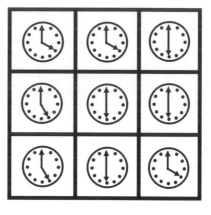

Answer 180
B.

Answer 181
H. Take the letter three before the given letter in alphabetical order (e.g., for D read A). If you also use the first letter of the given color you will get four five-letter words: apRil, brOwn, eaGle, nePal.

Answer 182
The colors are worth Green 4, Purple 5, Red 6, Orange 8. The formula is left side plus base, minus right side.

Answer 183
6. The colors are worth Yellow 1, Green 3, Pink 4, Orange 5, Red 6, Purple 9. Add the outer numbers and put the result in the opposite segment.

Answer 184
Yellow. The colors are worth Pink 2, Yellow 3, Orange 4, Green 5, Purple 6, Red 7, Brown 8. In each segment subtract the smaller of the outer numbers from the larger and put the result in the center of the next segment clockwise.

Answer 185
10. The colors are worth Orange 2, Red 3, Green 5, Yellow 6. The formula is 'add all three sides together'.

Answer 186
L. Take the letter after the one given. Use the first letters of the colors. You then get: biBle, rhYme, biRth, emPty.

Answer 187
The colors are in the sequence Orange, Yellow, Pink, Red, Green and form an inward spiral starting at the top left.

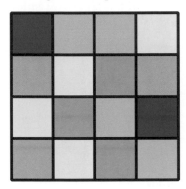

Answer 188
Bartok, Boulez, Chopin, Delius, Mahler.

Answer 189
A. Each shape increases by one of the same until there are three and it then becomes one. The image is reflected for a shape with two elements.

Answer 190
The pattern is +2 scales, +3 scales, –1 scale. A fish with an even number of scales faces the other way.

Answer 191
4.

Answer 192
B. The digits of all the others add up to 6.

Answer 193
D. The number of edges of the shapes in each square increases by 1 in each column, starting from the top.

Answer 194
16.

Answer 195
+ ÷ – x – +. The letters are based on their alphabetic position, so the sum would read: L(12) + D(4) ÷ B(2) – F(6) x K(11) – Q(17) + C(3) = H(8).

Answer 196
B.

Answer 197
3. The numbers rotate counterclockwise from one square to the next and decrease by 2 each time.

Answer 198
D.

Answer 199
9. Multiply the values in the same segments in wheels 2 and 3 and put the answer in the next segment in wheel 1, going clockwise.

Answer 200
JOL 1714. Go 5 forward and 3 back in the alphabet. The numbers continue from the alphabetic position of the letter.

Answer 201
G. Add 3 to odd numbers, subtract 2 from even numbers.

Answer 202
 Add the number of segments in column 1 to the number of segments in column 3. Draw this number of segments into column 2.

Answer 203
M. These are the letters with straight sides only.

Answer 204
Kebab, Pasta, Pizza, Tacos, Wurst.

Answer 205
E. Add two circles and two lines, take away one of each, repeat. The pattern is also rotated by 90° counterclockwise each time.

Answer 206
576. Multiply No. by speed, put the product as the distance for the next balloon.

Answer 207
A. Each ring contains one cross more than the previous example, and the first and last cross in each adjacent circle are level.

Answer 208
21. $\Delta = 12$, $* = 9$, $\heartsuit = 3$, $\% = 5$, $@ = 7$.

Answer 209
The pattern sequence is 7, 1, 1, 3, 2, 2, 5, 5, 4, 1. It starts at the top right and works in a counterclockwise spiral.

4	2	2
1	5	5
7	1	1

Answer 210
C.

Answer 211
G. It is a tempo; the others are dances.

Answer 212
21. Multiply each number by the number on the opposite side of the wheel on the same side of the spoke and put the product in that segment next to the center.

Answer 213
F. The circles and squares become squares and circles, respectively. The largest element loses all internal elements.

Answer 214
V. The letters are based on the number alphabet backwards (Z = 1, A = 26, etc.). The values on the bottom corners and the value in the middle added together result in the value on the apex.

Answer 215
Starting at opposite ends the symbols move alternately 1 and 2 steps to the other end of the grid in a boustrophedon.

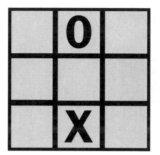

Answer 216
The corresponding sections in each wheel should contain a black section in each compartment.

Answer 217
D. Add consecutive clockwise corners of the diamond and place the sum on the corresponding second corner. Add the four numbers together and place the sum in the middle.

Answer 218
R. Starting on the top left hand corner, work through the alphabet, missing a letter each time, in a vertical boustrophedon.

Answer 219
No. 2. Take the first digit of the weight from the second to arrive at new number.

Answer 220
The pattern sequence is 1, 2, 2, 3, 4, 4, 1, 2, 3, 3, 4. Start at the top left and work in a horizontal boustrophedon.

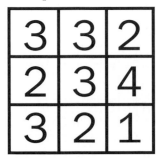

Answer 221
Camus, Defoe, Dumas, Verne, Wells.

Answer 222
1980. Vowels = 243, Consonants = 126

Answer 223
C. Convert each letter to its value based on its position in the alphabet. The values on each corner of a triangle added together result in the new letter in the middle.

Answer 224
A.

Answer 225
B. Each time the square becomes the circle, the triangle the square, and the circle the triangle.

Answer 226
Brunel, Darwin, Edison, Pascal, Planck.

Answer 227
C. Starting at the top right-hand corner, work through the alphabet, missing 1, 2, 3, 4, 5, 4, 3, 2, 1, 2, etc. letters each time, in a vertical boustrophedon.

Answer 228
3:13. Start time A minus Finish A equals Finish B. Start time B minus Finish B equals Finish C, etc.

Answer 229
92. Multiply the numbers on the diagonally opposite corners of each square and add the products. Put the sum in the third square along.

Answer 230
D. It is the only one to which a circle can be added where the triangle overlaps the circle and a right-angled line runs parallel to the whole of one side of the triangle.

Answer 231
B.

Answer 232
D. They are all in alphabetical order except for D.

Answer 233
3.

Answer 234
J. All of the others have a matching partner.

Answer 235
E. All elements consist of 3 straight lines except 'E', which consists of 4 straight lines.

Answer 236
The pattern sequence is @, @, %, *, %, &, &, *, %. It starts at the top right and works inwards in a counterclockwise spiral.

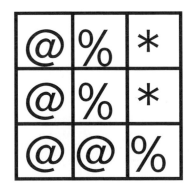

Answer 237
2.

Answer 238

61. Letters are worth the value based on alphabetical position (A=1, etc.). However, alternate letters are worth the value based on the reversed alphabet (A=26, etc.).

Answer 239

B.

Answer 240

Washington.

Answer 241

44. The numbers increase clockwise first missing one spoke, then two at the fourth step. Each circle increases by a different amount (2, 3, 4).

Answer 242

9. The numbers rotate clockwise and increase by 1 each time.

Answer 243

A. It is the only one to have an odd number of lines.

Answer 244

Bacon, Bosch, Klimt, Manet, Monet.

Answer 245

F. The small and large elements become large and small, respectively.

Answer 246

C. The number of small circles equals the number of edges of the shape, except for 'C', where there is one more circle than edges.

Answer 247

48. In each box of four numbers, multiply the top two numbers, put the product in the bottom right box, then subtract the top right number from the bottom right one and put the difference in the bottom left box.

Answer 248

C. The others are all in the correct order if you start from Earth and travel away from the sun.

Answer 249

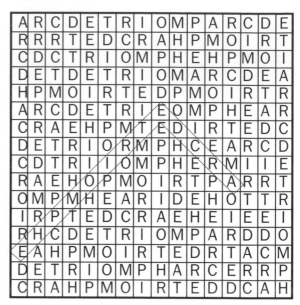

Answer 250

Starting with a vertical line reflect the dot first against that line and then each following line in a clockwise direction.

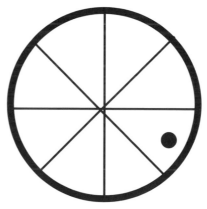

Answer 251

D. Each column of elements alternates and moves up two rows.

Answer 252

E. All the others consist of 3 consecutive letters in the alphabet.

Answer 253

Sly Sky. The name contains no vowels.

Answer 254
E. It is the only one where the small and large circles do not overlap.

Answer 255
10. Add 2 to each value, place sum in corresponding position in next triangle, then subtract 3, and add 2 again.

Answer 256
18. Multiply the numbers in the outer section, reverse the product and put it in the middle of the next section.

Answer 257
B. Working in a counterclockwise spiral pattern, in the first square there are eight lines, one missing, seven lines, one missing, etc. The number of lines before the first break decreases by one with each square.

Answer 258

Answer 259
F. This is based on the number alphabet backwards. Add together the corner squares of each row or column and put the sum in the middle square of the opposite row or column.

Answer 260
c). Add the digits to get the alphabetic number of the town's initial letter.

Answer 261
Blake, Byron, Dante, Donne, Plath.

Answer 262
B. Each arch moves closer to its opposite end by an equal amount each time.

Answer 263
1956. The numbers represent the leap years clockwise around the triangles starting at the apex. Miss one leap year each time.

Answer 264
20. Multiply hours by minutes and divide by 3 to get the number of the rider.

Answer 265
Forward, back, forward, back.

Answer 266
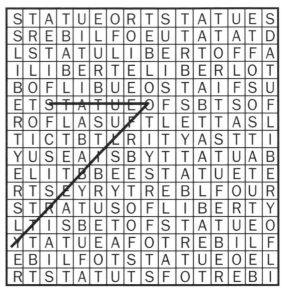

Answer 267
G. Starting at the bottom left corner, work through the alphabet in a counterclockwise spiral. Miss 1 letter, then 2 letters, 1 letter, etc., going back to the start of the alphabet after reaching Z.

Answer 268
9:05. The minute hand goes forward 25 minutes, the hour hand back by 5 hours.

Answer 269
13.

Answer 270
B. It is the only figure that does not have three boxes in one row.

Answer 271
C.

Answer 272
987. The tractor number is divided into the weight to give the acreage. The weights have been mixed up.

Answer 273

6. In each square, multiply the top and bottom left together, then multiply the top and bottom right. Subtract this second product from the first and put this number in the middle.

Answer 274

Add one leaf. Add two petals. Deduct 1 petal and add 1 leaf. Repeat.

Answer 275

384. Starting at the top right-hand corner work through the square in a vertical boustrophedon, multiplying by 4 and dividing by 2 alternately.

Answer 276

15. Take the minutes in the hours, add the minutes and divide by 10. Ignore the remainder.

Answer 277

S	E	R	E	P	E	N	S	T	I	N	E	R	E	S	E
E	E	S	E	N	R	P	E	N	S	E	R	P	E	N	T
R	S	R	S	E	I	S	R	T	E	R	P	E	N	T	I
P	E	P	P	S	E	T	P	I	N	E	N	E	S	S	S
E	R	E	S	N	T	N	N	E	R	I	N	N	N	N	E
N	P	N	E	R	T	E	T	E	P	N	S	E	E	I	R
T	E	T	R	P	S	I	I	T	T	P	T	R	T	P	
N	N	I	P	E	E	N	N	T	R	R	S	E	P	N	E
E	T	N	E	N	T	E	E	E	E	S	E	T	E	E	N
I	N	E	N	T	R	S	E	S	R	E	T	S	N	P	T
S	E	R	T	P	E	N	T	I	N	E	T	S	T	R	I
S	E	R	N	P	E	N	T	I	N	E	E	N	I	E	T
E	S	R	E	I	S	E	R	P	E	N	T	I	N	S	E
S	E	T	E	N	N	I	T	N	E	P	R	E	S	T	E
R	S	E	N	E	I	T	N	I	P	R	E	S	E	S	T
S	E	R	P	E	N	S	N	I	T	N	E	P	R	E	S

Answer 278

27. Add all the numbers for each square. For Yellow add 5, for Green subtract 5. Then swap the numbers in adjacent Yellow and Green squares.

Answer 279

14. The colors are worth Red 5, Yellow 3, Green 6, Blue 4. Add the sides together and swap the results within horizontally adjacent triangles.

Answer 280

11. The colors are worth Brown 1, Green 2, Orange 3, Yellow 4, Pink 5, Red 6, Purple 7. Add the outer numbers in each segment and place in the center of the next segment clockwise.

Answer 281

The sequence is Brown, Orange, Yellow, Brown, Purple, Green. It forms a diagonal boustrophedon (or ox plow pattern) starting in the bottom left corner.

Answer 282

14. Colors are worth Purple 2, Yellow 3, Orange 5, Green 6. Add sides together and put sum in center of triangle.

Answer 283

6. The colors are worth Red 1, Orange 2, Green 3, Yellow 4, Pink 5, Purple 6, Brown 7. Add the outer numbers and put the sum in the center of the opposite segment.

Answer 284

10. The colors are worth Pink 1, Green 2, Orange 3, Yellow 4, Red 5, Purple 6. In each segment subtract the smaller outer number from the larger and put the difference in the center of the next segment clockwise.

Answer 285

C. Each row and file must contain two Orange and two Green squares.

Hard Puzzles

PUZZLE 286

Take a letter from each cloud in turn. You will find the surnames of five film actors plus one extra name. Who is it?

Answer see page **248**

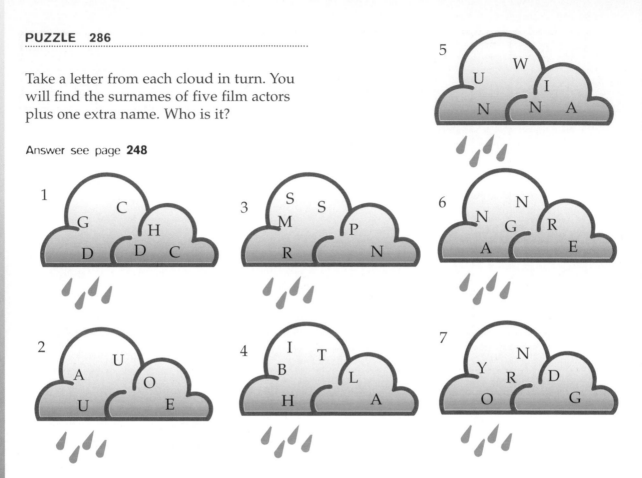

PUZZLE 287

Can you work out which symbol follows the series?

Answer see page **248**

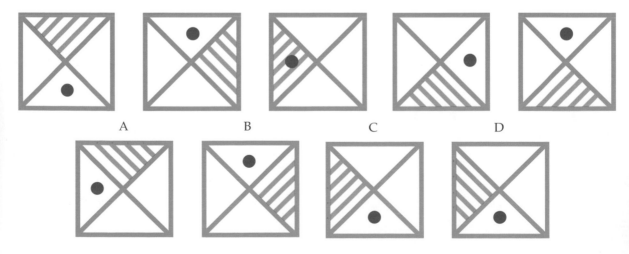

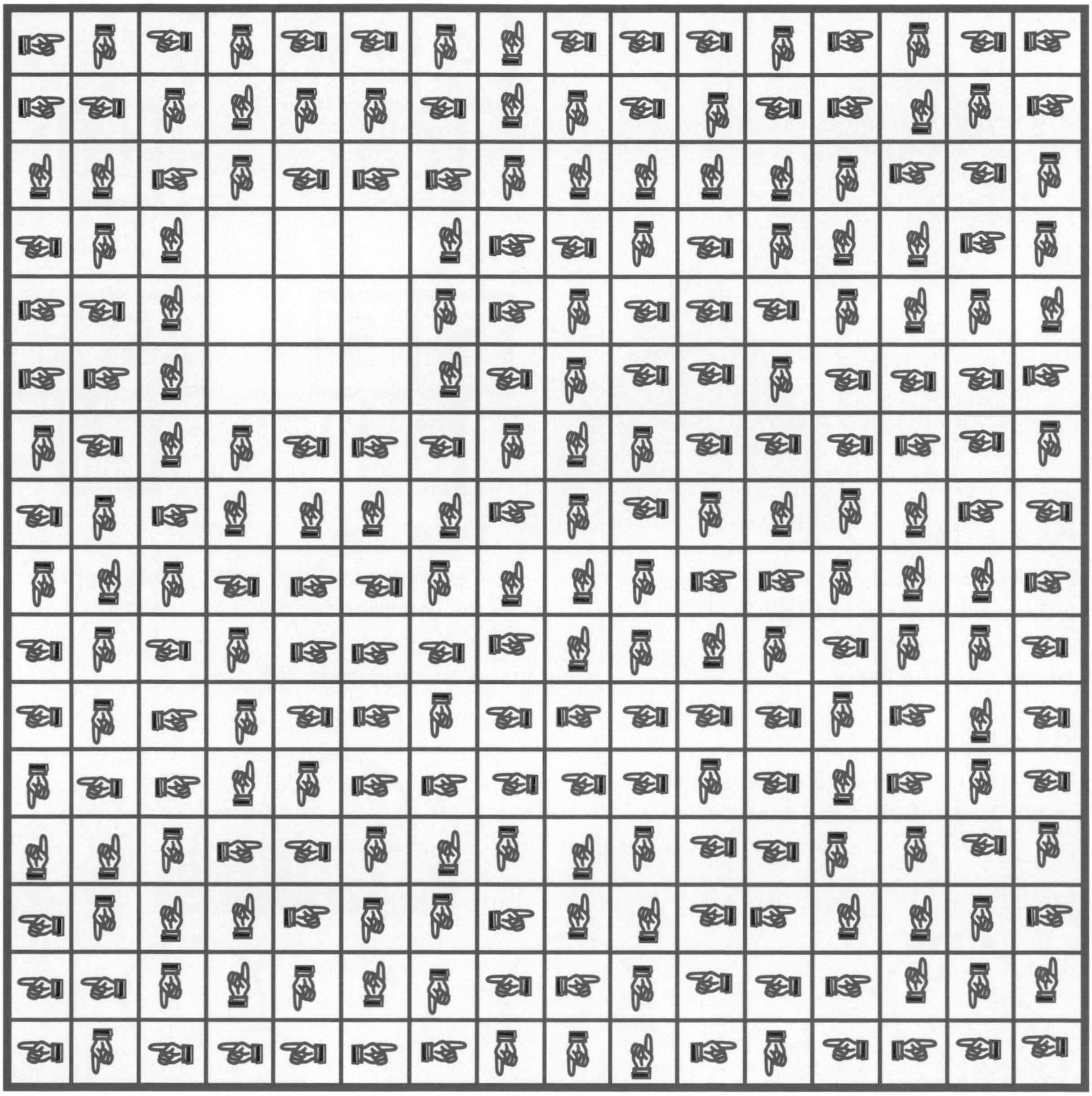

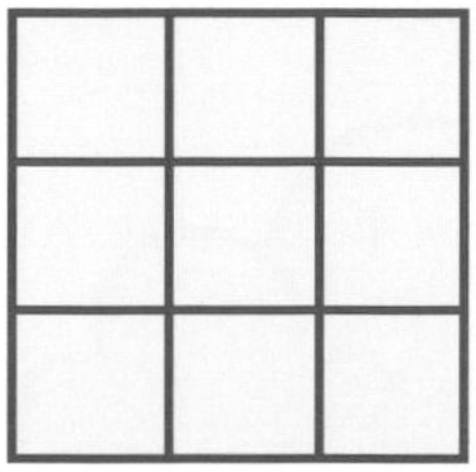

PUZZLE   288

Can you work out the reasoning behind this grid and complete the missing section?

Answer see page **248**

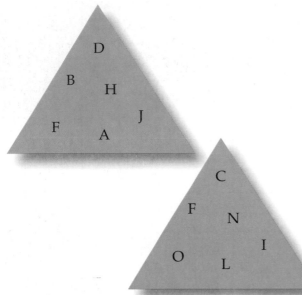

PUZZLE 289

Can you work out which are the two odd letters out in these triangles?

Answer see page **248**

PUZZLE 290

Can you work out what should replace the question mark?

Answer see page **248**

PUZZLE 291

Take a letter from each cloud in the given order. You will find the names of five composers and one extra name. Who is it?

Answer see page **248**

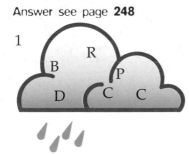

	1	2	3	4	5	6	7	8	9	10	11	12
1	S4	E3	SW2	E8	E3	E3	SE3	SW1	SW6	S6	S1	W2
2	SE4	S2	SE5	S2	NE1	S6	SE3	SE4	W5	SW2	S1	W11
3	NE1	E5	N2	E2	W1	SE3	S1	W5	S4	E2	NE1	W4
4	NE2	S3	W2	N3	E6	NW1	NW2	W5	N1	E2	S3	W7
5	E2	SW1	NE4	SW1	S2	S2	W5	W1	W4	SE1	✳	W1
6	E3	NE4	E7	SW2	E2	N2	SE2	N4	N1	N4	N5	S2
7	E6	N1	E9	NE2	NE1	NE3	NE1	NW6	W5	N4	W10	N2
8	NE3	N5	NE6	E4	W2	W2	E3	W1	W4	E1	NW3	W11

PUZZLE 292

This diagram represents a treasure map. You are allowed to stop on each square only once (though you may cross a square as often as you like). When you stop on a square you must follow the instructions you find there. The first one or two letters stand for points of the compass (N = North, S = South, etc.), the number stands for the number of steps you have to take. The finishing point is the square with the asterisk.

Can you find the starting point? There is one complication. You will find that you never land on some of the squares at all. If you cross out those squares on which you have landed you will see that those on which you have not landed form a two-figure number. What is it?

Answer see page **248**

PUZZLE 293

Can you work out the reasoning behind this diagram and fill in the last square?

Answer see page **248**

PUZZLE 294

Can you work out what the missing symbol should look like?

Answer see page **248**

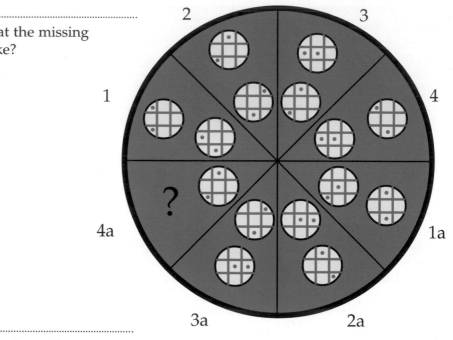

PUZZLE 295

These letters, when joined together correctly, make up a novel and its author. Can you spot it?

Answer see page **248**

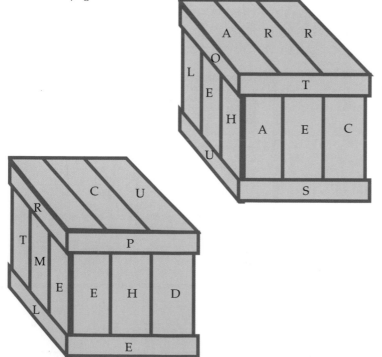

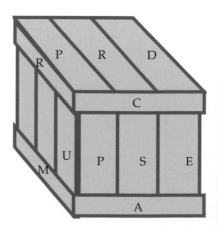

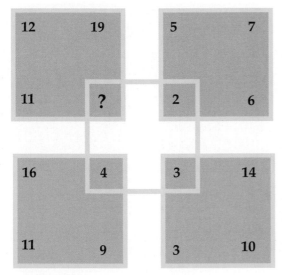

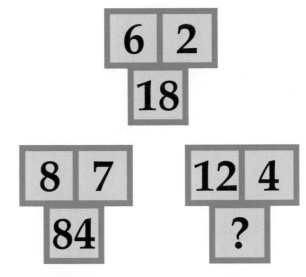

PUZZLE 296

Can you find the number that should replace the question mark?

Answer see page **248**

PUZZLE 297

Can you work out what number should replace the question mark?

Answer see page **248**

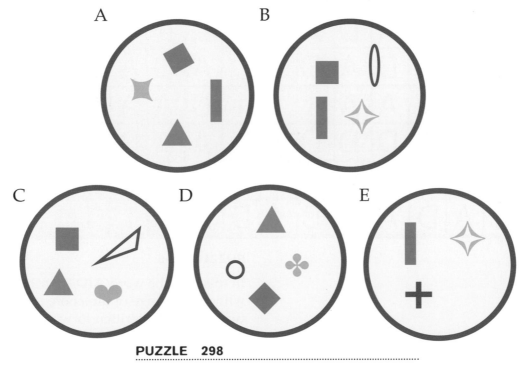

PUZZLE 298

Can you find the odd one out?

Answer see page **248**

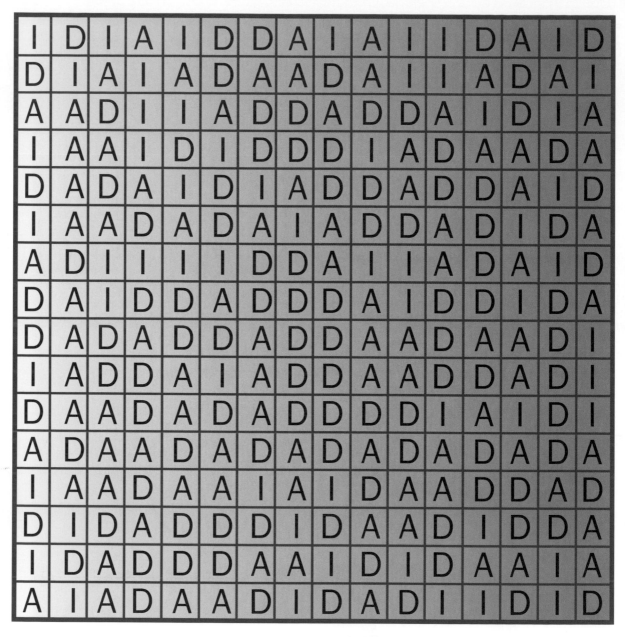

PUZZLE 299

In this grid the word AIDA, written without a change of direction, appears twice. It can be written forwards and backwards in a horizontal, vertical or diagonal direction. Can you spot it both times?

Answer see page **249**

PUZZLE 300

Can you unravel the reasoning behind this star and fill in the missing letter?

Answer see page **249**

PUZZLE 301

Can you work out what number the missing hour hand on clock 4 should point at?

Answer see page **249**

A

Boston – Nashville

B

Chicago – Vancouver

C

Houston – Toronto

D

Cleveland – Richmond

E

Augusta – ?

    a) Washington
    b) Milwaukee
    c) Ottawa
    d) Galveston

PUZZLE 302

Can you unravel the logic behind the starting point and destination of each of these cars and find out where car E is going?

Answer see page **249**

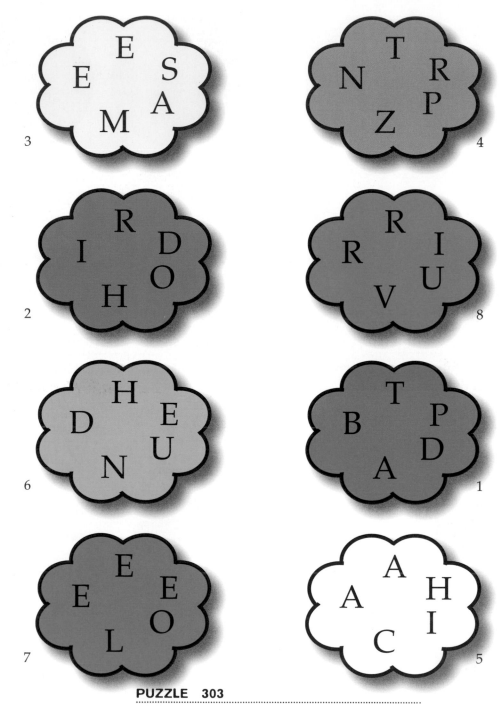

PUZZLE   303

Pick one letter from each flower in the order shown. You will get the names of five statesmen. Who are they?

Answer see page **249**

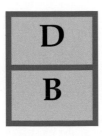

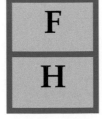

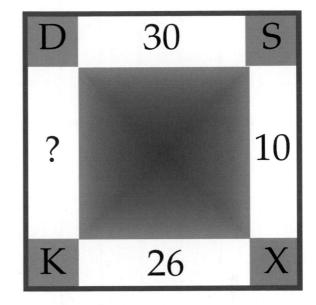

PUZZLE 304

Can you unravel the reasoning behind these domino pieces and find the missing letter?

Answer see page **249**

PUZZLE 305

Can you work out what number should replace the question mark?

Answer see page **249**

14   ?   29

PUZZLE 306

Can you work out what number fits underneath letter A?

Answer see page **249**

		2	7	3	8	4	9		2	7	3	8	4	9
9	9								2	7	3	8	4	9
4	4	3	8	4	9									
8	8	7			2	7	3	8	4	9				
3	3	2		4	9									
7	7			8	7	3	8	4	9				2	
2	2			3	2								7	
				7									3	
				2									8	2
													4	7
9													9	3
4														8
8					9	4	8	3	7	2				4
3					9	4	8	3	7	2				9
7		9	4	8	3	7	2							
2					9	4	8	3	7	2				

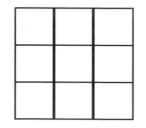

PUZZLE 307

The numbers in this grid occur in the following order: 9, 4, 8, 3, 7, 2 and run in a counterclockwise spiral starting at the top right. It is complicated by the addition of spaces and repeats according to a pattern. Can you complete the missing section?

Answer see page **249**

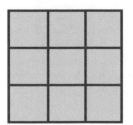

PUZZLE 308

Can you work out the reasoning behind this grid and complete the missing section?

Answer see page **249**

PUZZLE 309

Can you unravel the reasoning behind this juggler and find the missing letter?

Answer see page **249**

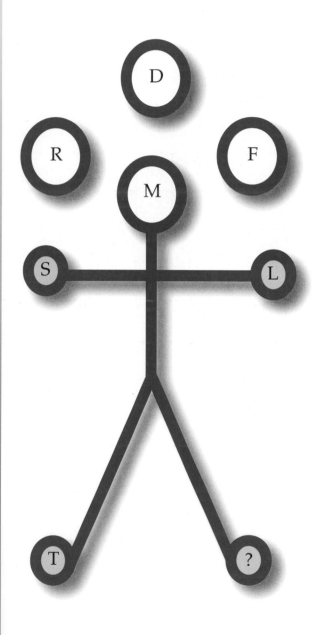

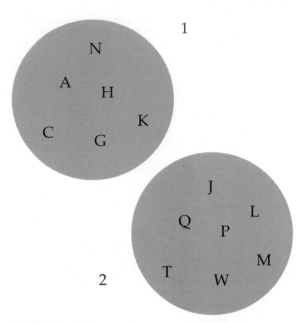

1

2

PUZZLE 310

Can you work out what letter does not belong in the second circle?

Answer see page **249**

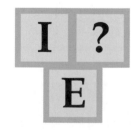

PUZZLE 311

Can you work out what letter fits the square with the question mark?

Answer see page **249**

186

PUZZLE 312

The four pieces below, when fitted together correctly, form a circle. However, one has gone missing. Can you find which of the lower four it is?

Answer see page 249

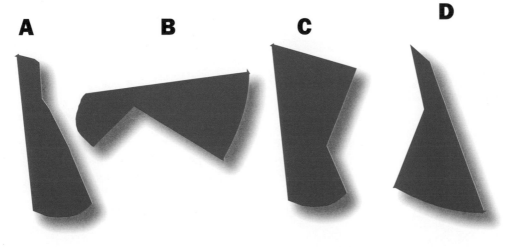

A   B   C   D

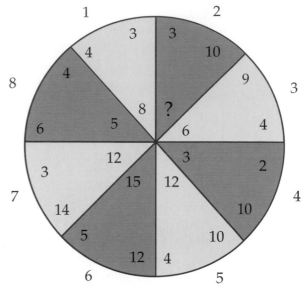

PUZZLE 313

Can you unravel the reasoning behind this grid and complete the missing square?

Answer see page **250**

PUZZLE 314

Can you find the missing number in this wheel?

Answer see page **250**

PUZZLE 315

Take a letter from each cloud in turn. You should find the names of five painters and one extra name. What is it?

Answer see page **250**

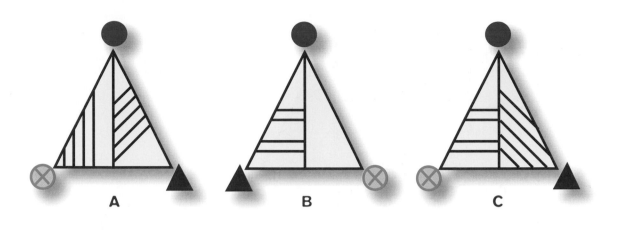

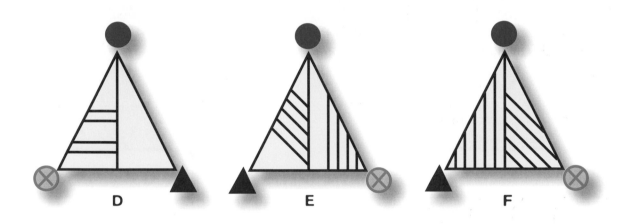

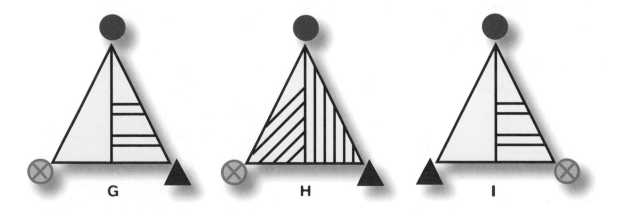

PUZZLE 316

....

Can you work out which is the odd one out?

Answer see page **250**

PUZZLE 317

Can you unravel the logic behind these diagrams and find the missing letter?

Answer see page **250**

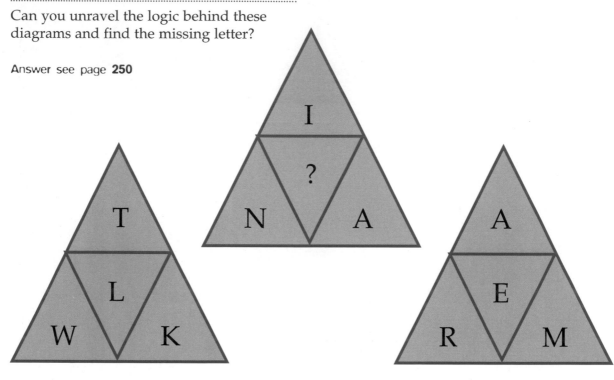

PUZZLE 318

Can you find the letter that should replace the question mark?

Answer see page **250**

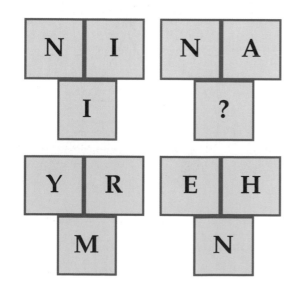

PUZZLE 319

Can you work out what the missing number is?

Answer see page **250**

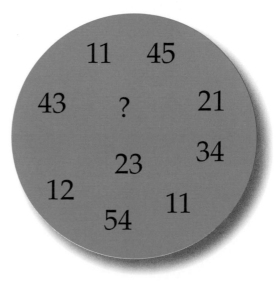

D	R	I	V	E	R	I	D	V	E	R	D	D	R	I	V
R	D	R	I	V	E	R	D	R	I	V	E	R	V	E	R
I	V	E	R	D	V	E	R	D	D	R	I	V	E	R	V
V	D	R	I	V	E	R	D	E	R	C	I	E	V	V	E
E	D	R	I	V	E	E	R	V	D	I	V	E	R	D	R
D	R	I	V	E	V	R	V	D	E	R	I	V	E	R	D
V	D	E	R	I	D	I	V	E	R	D	R	I	V	E	R
D	R	I	R	V	E	R	D	R	I	D	R	D	V	D	E
D	R	R	V	I	D	R	E	V	E	R	D	R	I	V	E
D	A	D	R	I	V	E	D	R	I	V	D	R	I	V	E
I	R	D	R	E	V	I	R	D	R	E	V	I	R	D	R
V	E	R	D	D	R	I	V	E	R	D	R	I	V	E	D
V	I	V	I	V	E	V	R	D	E	V	D	E	V	I	R
E	R	E	R	E	D	E	D	R	R	I	R	V	E	R	I
R	D	R	D	R	R	R	R	I	D	R	I	I	R	D	V
I	I	I	D	I	D	E	V	I	D	V	R	D	R	E

PUZZLE 320

In this grid the name VERDI appears in its entirety only once in a straight line. Can you spot it? However, there is also another word hidden which involves one change of direction. What is it? It might have been one of the composer's famous last words.

Answer see page **250**

191

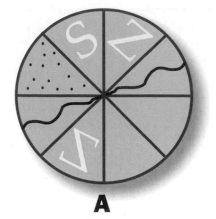

A

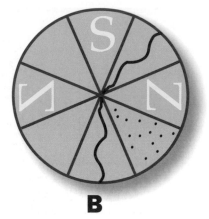

B

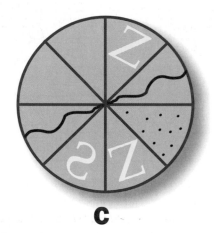

C

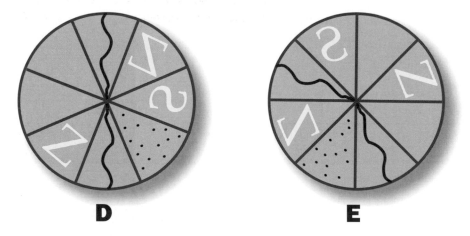

D

E

PUZZLE 321

Can you work out which is the odd
diagram out?

Answer see page **250**

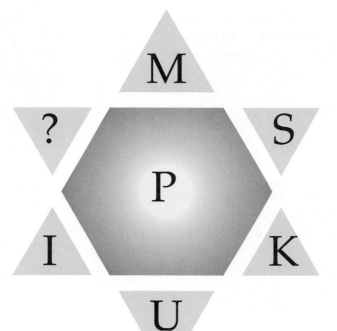

PUZZLE 322

Can you unravel the reasoning behind this star and fill in the missing letter?

Answer see page **250**

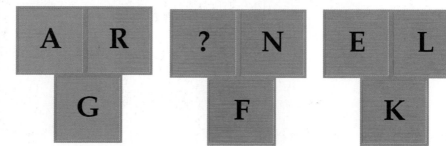

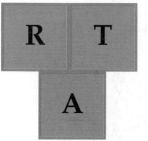

PUZZLE 323

Can you work out what letter fits in the square with the question mark?

Answer see page **250**

3

5

1

4

7

2

8

6

PUZZLE 324

Pick one letter from each flower in the
order shown. You will get the
names of five actors.

Answer see page **250**

PUZZLE 325

Can you work out which two models cannot be made from the above layout?

Answer see page **250**

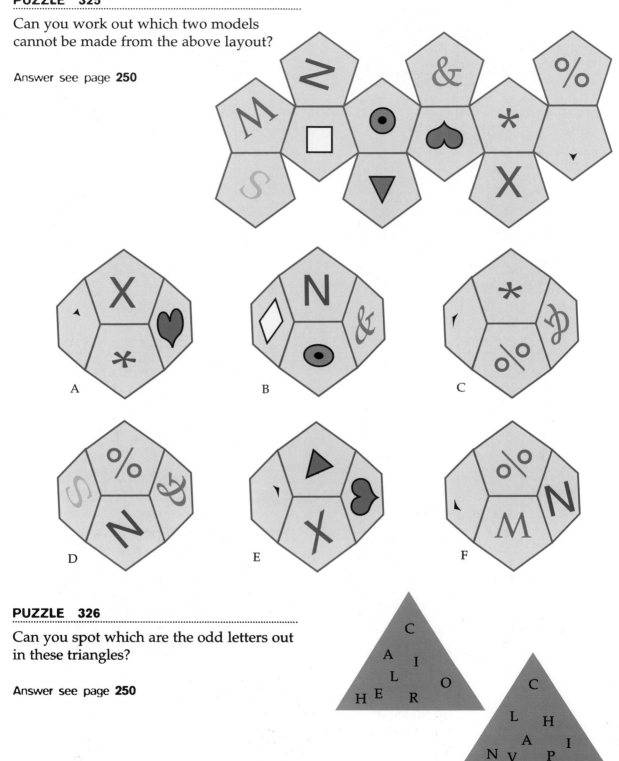

A

B

C

D

E

F

PUZZLE 326

Can you spot which are the odd letters out in these triangles?

Answer see page **250**

6	G	B	6	2	G	F	5
5	D	3	9	D	I	3	4
1	F	7	H	A	7	1	H
9	E	4	C	2	5	C	E
2	A	6	G	8	I	F	8
8	I	5			B	1	4
3	B	1			H	9	E
7	H	9	E	4	C	2	A
4	C	2	A	6	G	8	I
6	G	8	I	5	D	3	B
A	D	3	B	1	F	7	H
H	5	7	H	9	E	4	C
6	2	F	C	2	A	6	G
8	D	I	4	8	I	5	D
A	B	7	1	G	B	1	F
F	5	9	C	E	3	9	E

PUZZLE 327

This grid follows the pattern: 5, 6, 4, 7, 3, 8, 2, 9, 1, with the letters (in their positions in the alphabet) alternately replacing numbers. Can you fill the missing section?

Answer see page 251

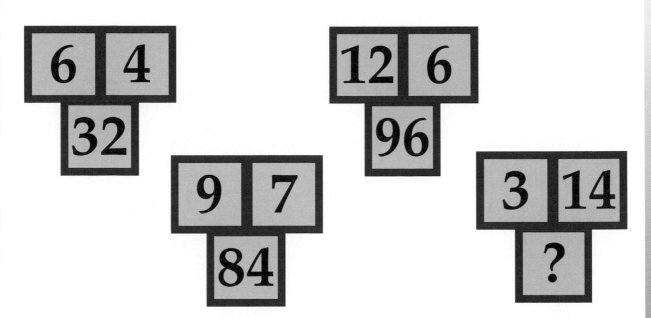

PUZZLE 328

Can you work out what number should go into the square with the question mark?

Answer see page **251**

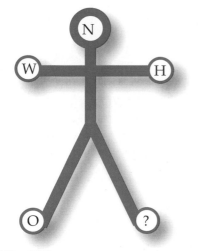

PUZZLE 329

Can you replace the question mark with a letter?

Answer see page **251**

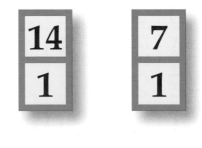

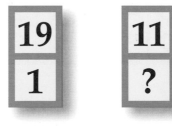

PUZZLE 330

Can you find the missing number on the domino piece? You will find the answer in Japan.

Answer see page **251**

5	3	6	4	4	3	5	7	5	7	9	2	2	5	8	3
9	8	9	6	1	5	8	6	6	8	3	7	6	7	4	4
2	1	5	7	8	3	1	3	5	1	6	6	8	9	8	6
7	6	2	9	1	1	8	3	1	5	1	7	5	3	4	1
8	5	6	6	2	4	4	8	3	8	4	7	1	6	1	8
7	6	2	2	5	2	3	7	4	5	8	5	7	6	3	1
7	9	3	1	8	4	5	4	7	7	9	4	8	5	6	3
3	6	8	8	2	9	8	8	2	5	7	2	1	8	3	5
5	6	9	6	5	3	4	7	4	7	4	2	6	6	5	5
1	6	3	2	3	4	5	8	1	1	2	4	9	3	2	7
5	8	9	7	1	8	3	6	9	3	6	3	5	4	9	4
8	4	5	6	7	1	5	1	8	5	8	3	1	2	5	7
7	2	2	9	2	2	4	7	4	9	4	1	8	6	7	8
2	4	3	9	5	6	7	8	5	8	3	2	7	5	6	1
5	9	4	3	4	2	6	1	7	3	4	9	2	6	9	1
3	2	5	8	1	3	2	5	3	8	3	5	3	1	2	7

PUZZLE   331

Look at this grid carefully and you will find pairs of numbers that add up to 10, in a either horizontal, vertical or diagonal direction. How many can you spot?

Answer see page **251**

PUZZLE 332

Pick one letter from each cloud in the order shown. You will find the names of five playwrights plus one extra name. Who is it?

Answer see page **251**

PUZZLE 333

Can you work out the reasoning behind this wheel and fill in the missing number?

Answer see page **251**

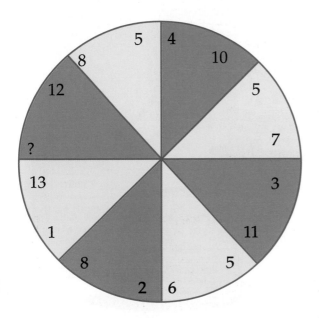

PUZZLE 334

Can you replace the question mark with a number?

Answer see page **251**

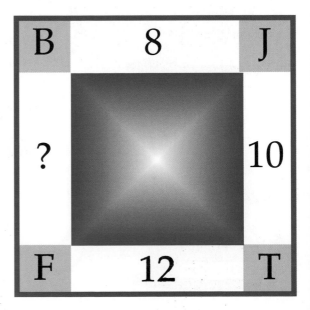

PUZZLE 335

Can you unravel the reasoning behind this square and replace the question mark with a number?

Answer see page **251**

3	6	3	5
4	12	11	1
3	?	15	5
1	6	7	2

PUZZLE 336

Each of the cars was filled with fuel. Can you unravel the connection between the licence plate and amount of fuel and work out what amount the last car was filled with?

A) 30 units   B) 72 units
C) 36 units   D) 78 units

Answer see page **251**

51 units
C275 MAZ

26 units
B496 LXY

43 units
F287 PTF

59 units
A194 HCW

? units
K948 SGN

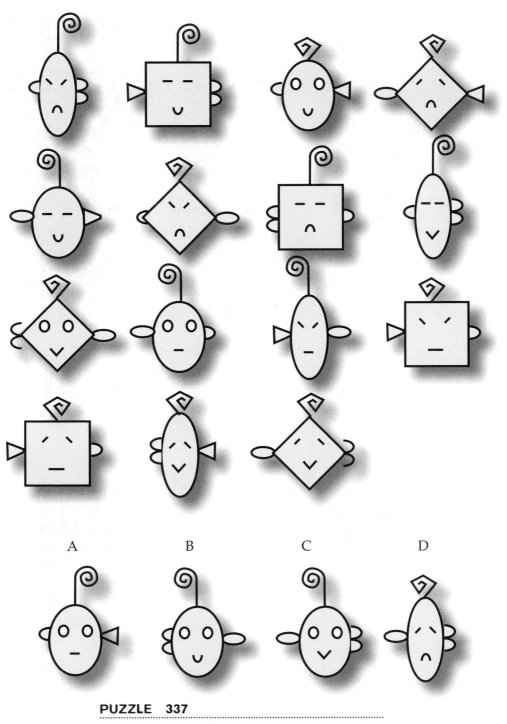

A   B   C   D

PUZZLE 337

Can you work out which face would fit the
missing space?

Answer see page **251**

6	7	3	8	2	4	1	6	9	5	91
3	4	6	2	9	7	7	6	3	4	111
5	9	6	8	3	2	4	7			74
9	8	2	3			6	8			51
8	7	3	4			6	1	4	6	68
2	9	5	4	8	3	6	2	7	8	97
4	3	2	9	1	4	5	6	8	3	85
6	2	4	3	1	7	9	6	3	8	91
2	4	7	6			1	2			36
3	5	6	8			2	4			45

90 108 89 100 36 44 94 82 52 ?

PUZZLE 338

Find a number that could replace the question mark. Each color represents a number under 10. Some may be negative numbers.

Answer see page **251**

103   131   135   107

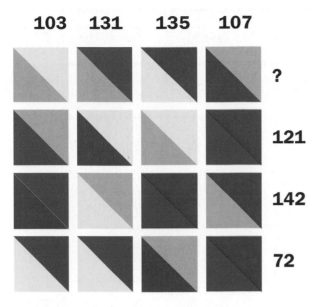

?

121

142

72

-13   19   17   19

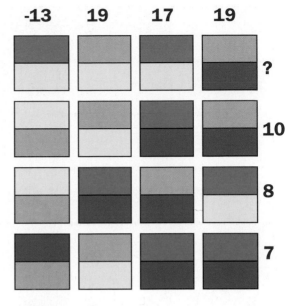

?

10

8

7

PUZZLE 339

Find a number that could replace the question mark. Each color represents a number under 10.

Answer see page **251**

PUZZLE 340

Find a letter that could replace the question mark.

Answer see page **251**

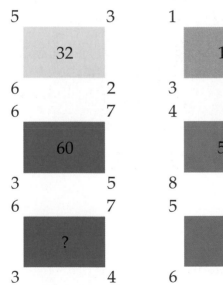

5   3
32
6   2

6   7
60
3   5

6   7
?
3   4

1   4
11
3   4

4   9
54
8   3

5   9
?
6   5

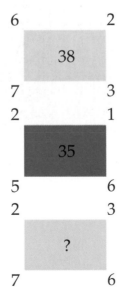

6   2
38
7   3

2   1
35
5   6

2   3
?
7   6

7   3
20
4   1

7   3
29
4   3

8   4
?
3   6

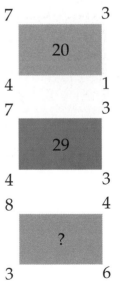

PUZZLE 341

What numbers should replace the question marks?

Answer see page **251**

3	4	6	9	7	2	5	8	3	9	?
6	5	2	7	3	4	5	1	2	6	71
3	8	2	1	9	7	8	6	1	3	82
5	4	3	4	1	2	9	8	6	5	85
6	8	9	3	5	4	8	3	6	2	91
4	1	9	8	6	3	2	2	4	5	74
7	6	3	5	2	4	6	8	9	7	93
8	4	6	5	3	6	2	1	3	8	83
9	2	1	4	3	7	8	9	6	3	88
1	3	7	6	4	3	8	6	2	4	77
89	75	77	87	79	86	81	93	67	102	

PUZZLE 342

Find a number that could replace the question mark. Each color represents a number under 10.

Answer see page **252**

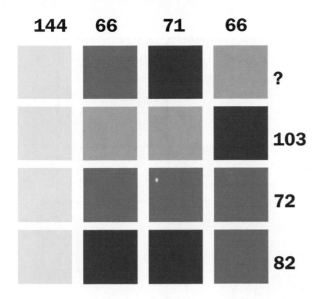

144   66   71   66

?

103

72

82

PUZZLE 343

Find a number that could replace the question mark. Each color represents a number under 10.

Answer see page **252**

PUZZLE 344

If you start at the left-most segment, blue, what is the color of the segment that should replace the question mark?

Answer see page **252**

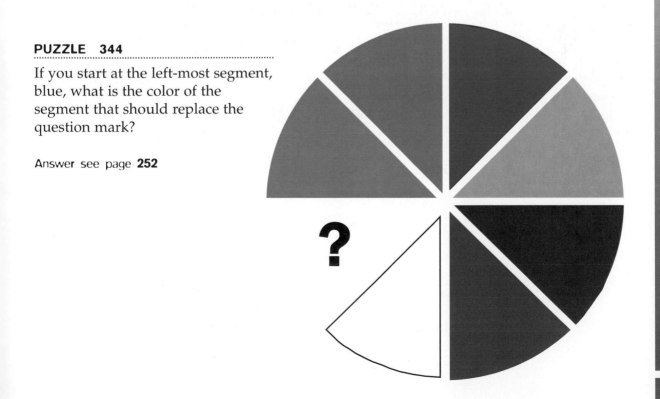

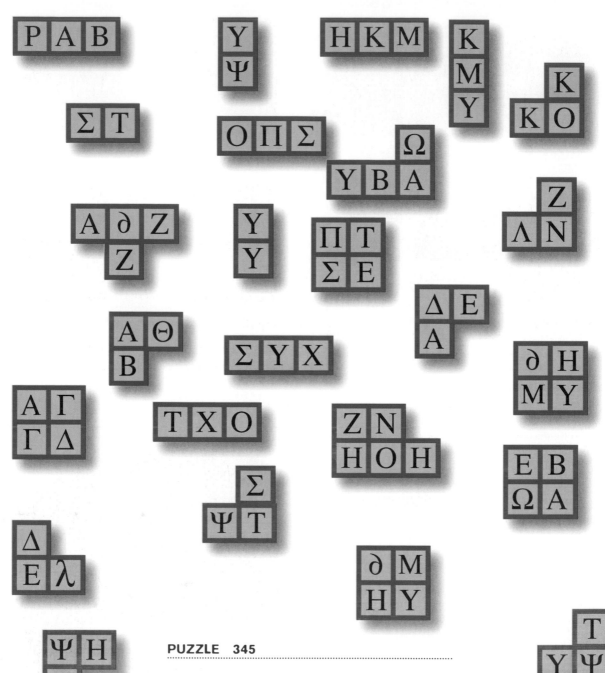

PUZZLE 345

These tiles, when placed in the right order, will form a square in which each horizontal line is identical with one vertical line. Can you successfully form the square?

Answer see page **252**

1 **2**

3 **4**

PUZZLE 346

Can you work out what the last clockface should look like?

Answer see page **252**

PUZZLE 347

Can you work out what is the missing letter on the last domino piece?

Answer see page **252**

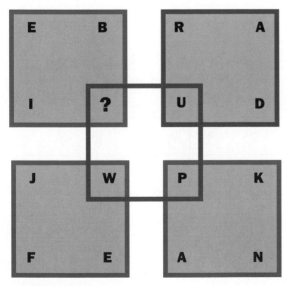

PUZZLE 348

Can you unravel the reasoning behind this diagram and find the missing letter?

Answer see page **252**

628

718

410

606

325

426

549

PUZZLE 349

Can you find the odd number out?

Answer see page **252**

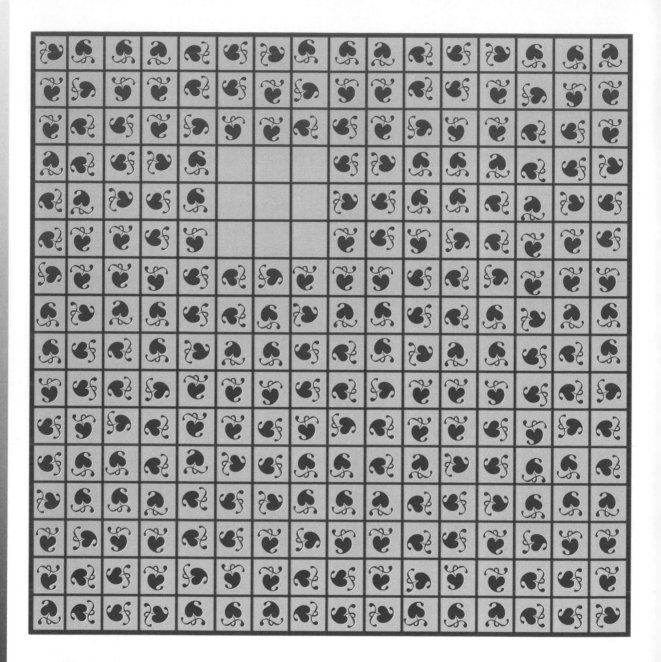

PUZZLE 350

Can you work out the reasoning behind this grid and fill in the missing section?

Answer see page **252**

PUZZLE 351

Can you find the missing letter?

Answer see page **252**

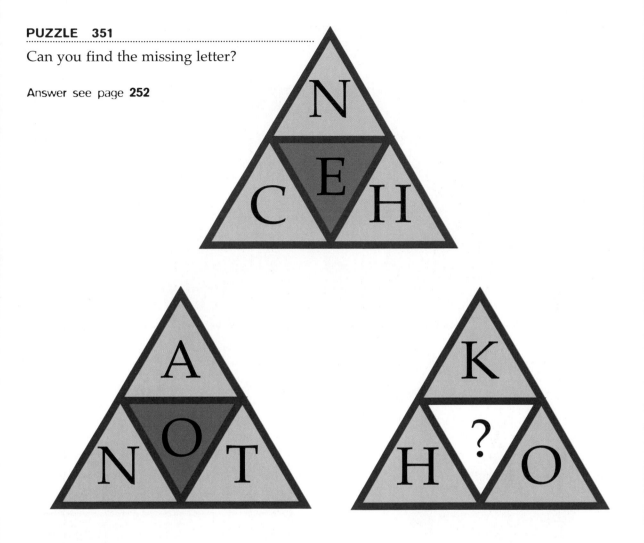

PUZZLE 352

Can you unravel the reasoning behind
these diagrams and find the
missing letter?

Answer see page **252**

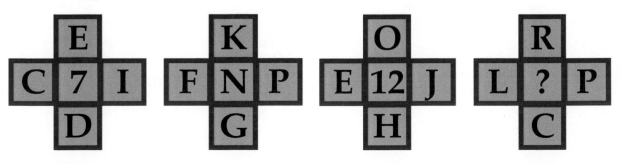

PUZZLE 353

Can you unravel the pattern of this wheel
and find the missing element?

Answer see page **252**

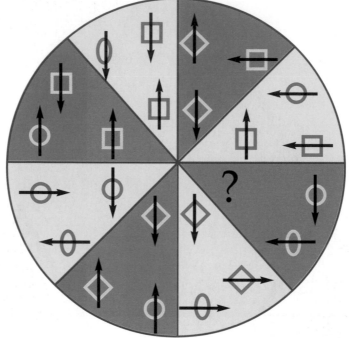

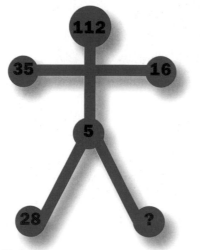

PUZZLE 354

Can you unravel the reasoning behind this
diagram and find the missing number?

Answer see page **252**

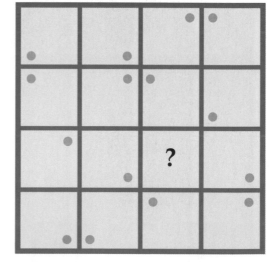

PUZZLE 355

Can you work out what the square with
the question mark should look like?

Answer see page **252**

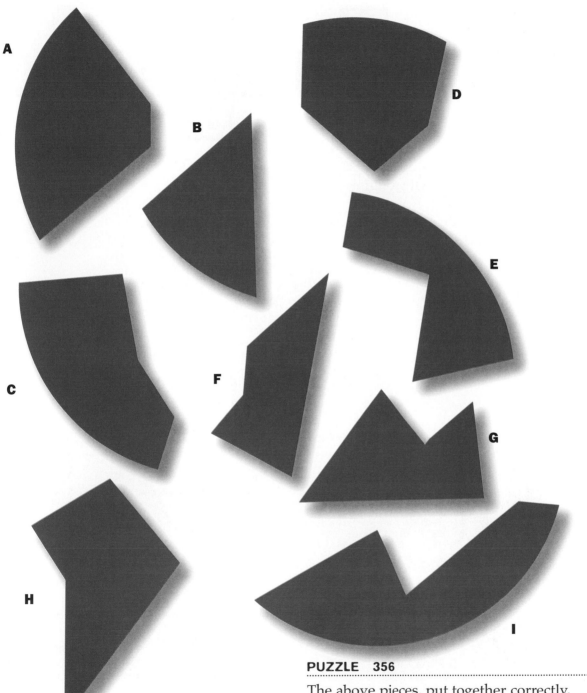

PUZZLE 356

The above pieces, put together correctly, form a circle. However, two extra pieces got mixed up with them which are not part of the disc. Can you find them?

Answer see page **253**

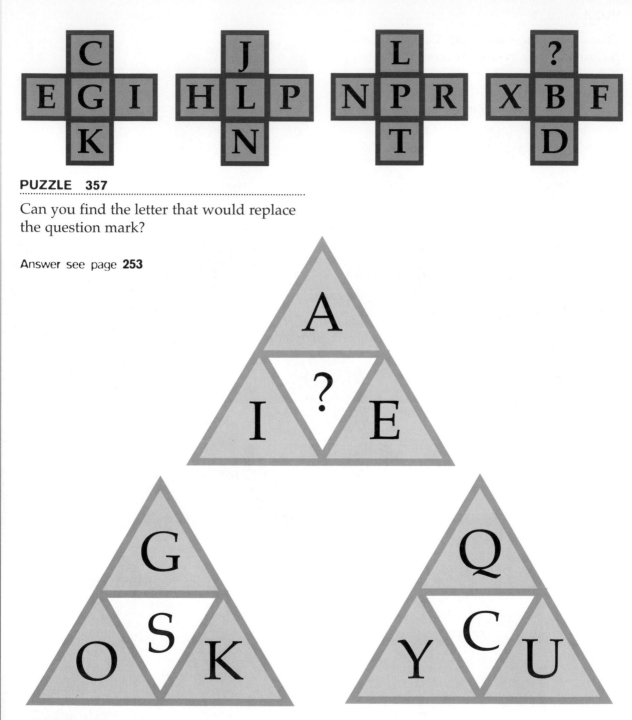

PUZZLE 357

Can you find the letter that would replace the question mark?

Answer see page **253**

PUZZLE 358

Can you unravel the logic behind these diagrams and find the missing letter?

Answer see page **253**

PUZZLE 359

The above pieces make up a circle when put together correctly. However, one piece is missing. Which is it?

Answer see page **253**

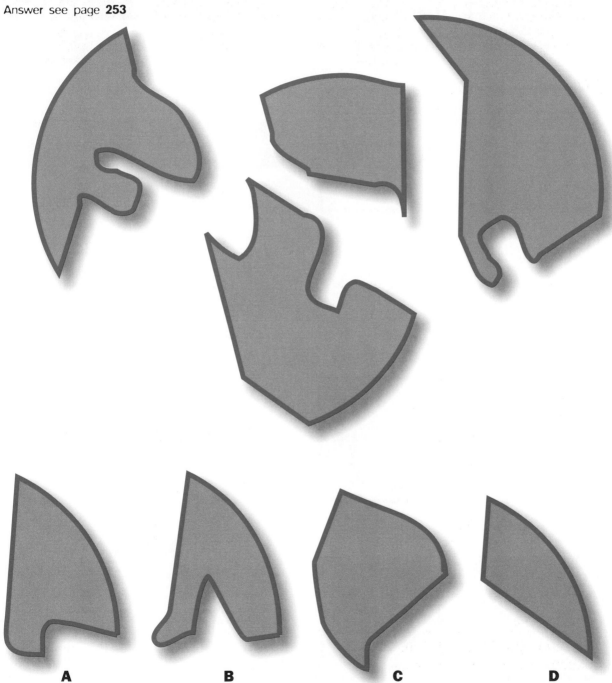

A   B   C   D

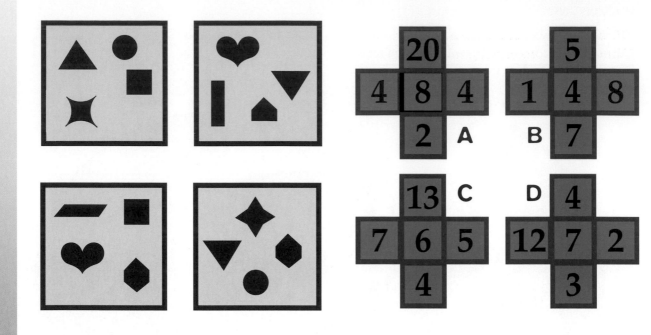

PUZZLE 360

Can you work out which diagram would follow the series above?

Answer see page **253**

PUZZLE 361

Can you work out which is the odd diagram out?

Answer see page **253**

A

B

C

D

PUZZLE 362

Can you work out what is the missing letter?

Answer see page **253**

PUZZLE 363

Can you find the missing number?

Answer see page 253

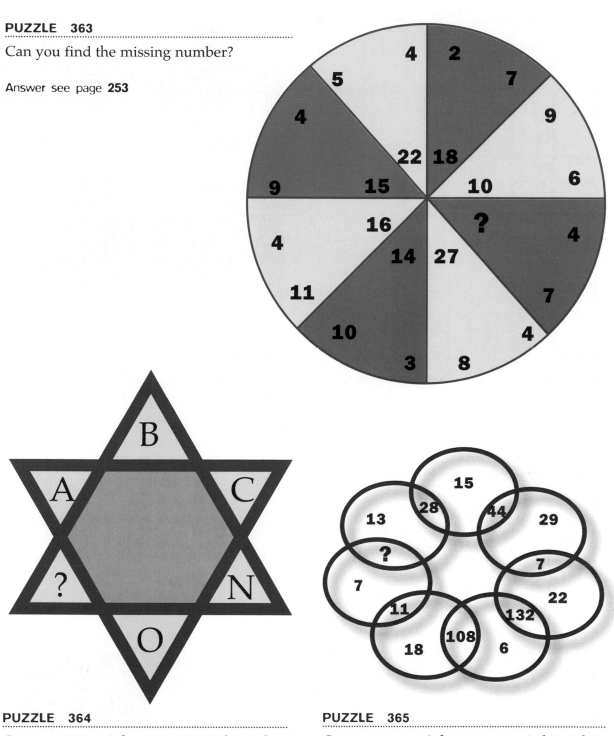

PUZZLE 364

Can you unravel the reasoning behind this star and find the missing letter?

Answer see page 253

PUZZLE 365

Can you unravel the reasoning behind this diagram and find the missing number?

Answer see page 253

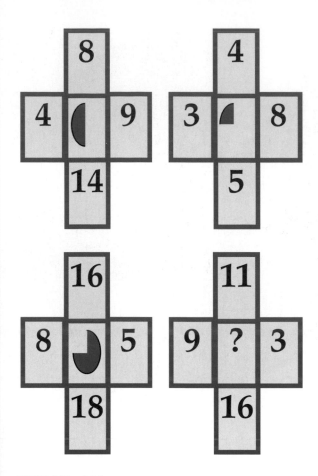

1	1	5	2	1	8	4	3
1	4	4	1	8	3	5	1
1	4	2	2	5	6	7	1
1	4	2	3	3	1	1	2
1	4	2	3	7	7	3	4
4	4	2	4	8	2	2	7
3	1	2	3	7	2	8	8
8	7	4	3	7	2	8	5
1	5	3	7	7	2	8	5
5	3	2	8	2	2	8	5
2	1	7	4	5	8	8	5
7	8	4	2	1	1	5	5

PUZZLE 366

Can you unravel the reasoning behind these diagrams and find the missing shape?

Answer see page **253**

PUZZLE 367

This grid follows the pattern: 3, 1, 4, 1, 5, 8, 2, 7. As a complication you will find some numbers have been increased by one. If you highlight these numbers you will discover a letter. What is it?

Answer see page **253**

PUZZLE 368

Can you work out which is the odd number out in each circle?

Answer see page **253**

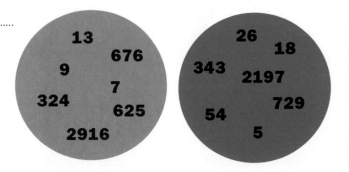

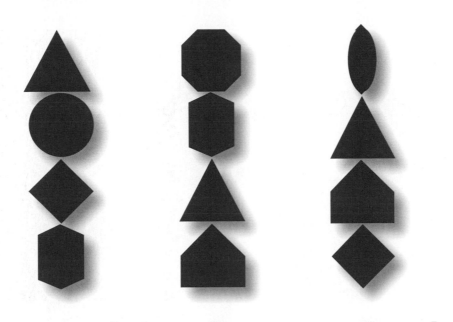

A   is to   B   as   C   is to:

D   E   F   G

PUZZLE   369

Answer see page **253**

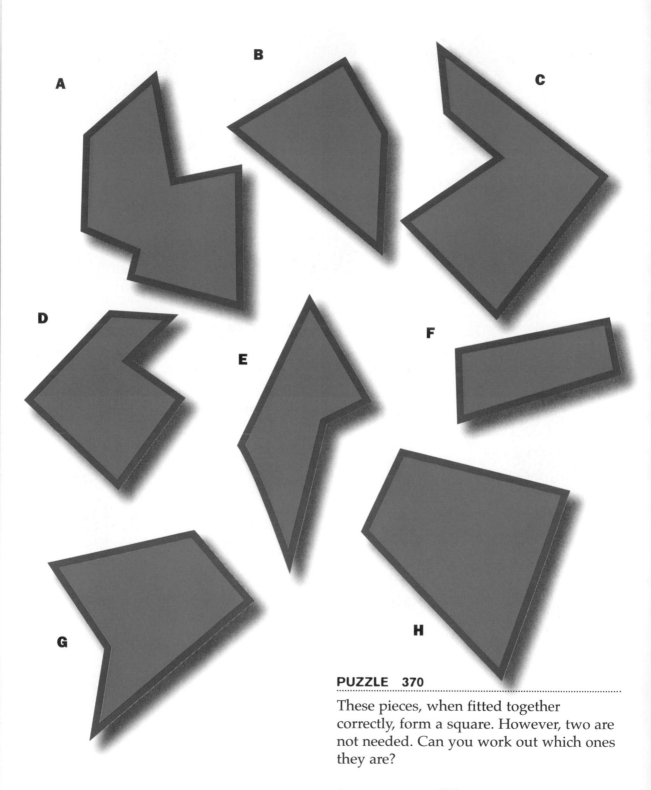

A

B

C

D

E

F

G

H

PUZZLE 370

These pieces, when fitted together correctly, form a square. However, two are not needed. Can you work out which ones they are?

Answer see page **253**

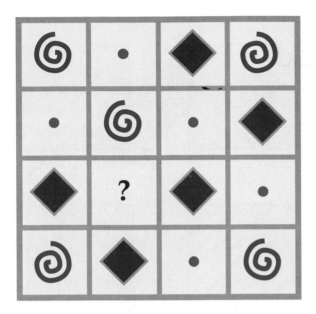

PUZZLE 371

Can you work out which shape should replace the question mark in this square?

Answer see page **253**

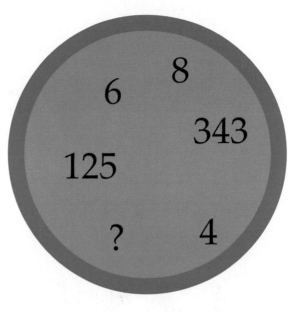

PUZZLE 372

Can you work out what number is missing from this circle?

Answer see page **253**

32   41   ?

PUZZLE 373

Can you find the number that fits below the 7?

Answer see page **253**

PUZZLE 374

Can you unravel the logic behind this diagram and find the missing number?

Answer see page **254**

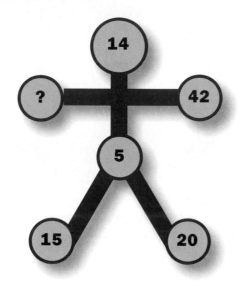

PUZZLE 375

Can you unravel the reasoning behind this wheel and replace the question mark with a number?

Answer see page **254**

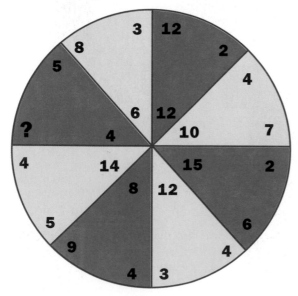

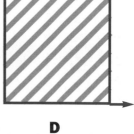

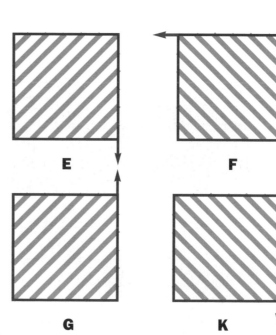

PUZZLE 376

Can you work out which diagram is the odd one out?

Answer see page **254**

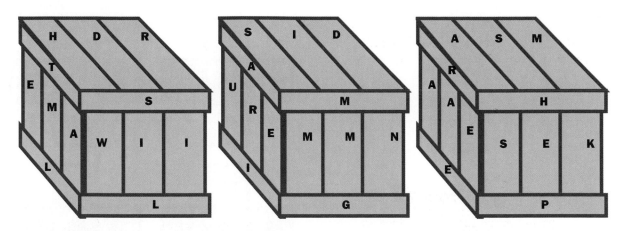

PUZZLE 377

A well-known work of literature and its author are concealed in these crates. What are they?

Answer see page **254**

PUZZLE 378

These pieces, when fitted together correctly, make up a square. However, one piece is not needed. Can you work out which one it is?

Answer see page **254**

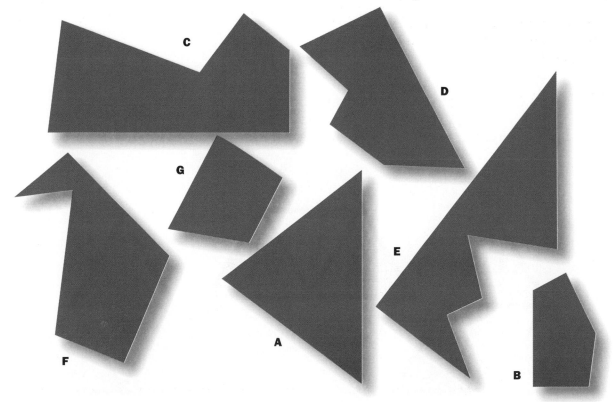

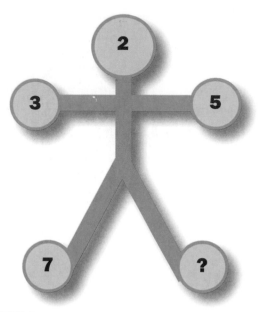

PUZZLE 379

Can you work out what number would replace the question mark?

Answer see page **254**

PUZZLE 380

Can you spot the odd one out?

Answer see page **254**

PUZZLE 381

Can you unravel the reasoning behind these diagrams and find the missing letter?

Answer see page **254**

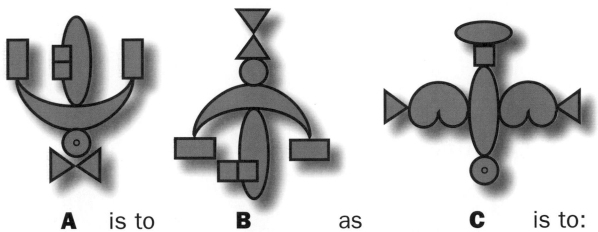

A   is to   **B**   as   **C**   is to:

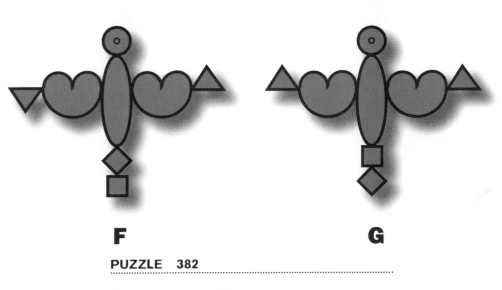

D   **E**

F   **G**

PUZZLE 382

Answer see page **254**

PUZZLE 383

Can you work out which two models
cannot be made from the above layout?

Answer see page **254**

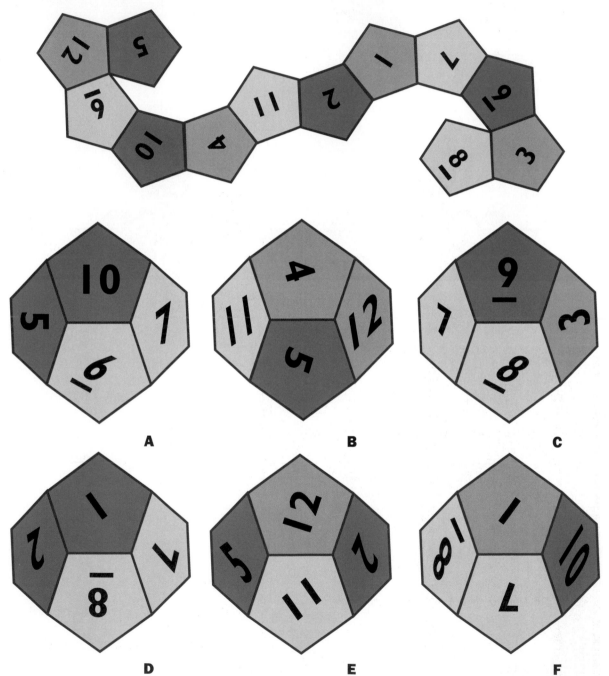

A

B

C

D

E

F

PUZZLE 384

Can you find the odd number out?

Answer see page 254

19

91

11

17

23

53

41

3 3 9 3

5 8 2 1

4 3 8 1

8 2 1 ?

PUZZLE 385

This square follows a pattern. Can you unravel it and replace the question mark with a number?

Answer see page 254

PUZZLE 386

The above pieces, when fitted together correctly, form a square. However, one wrong piece is among them. Can you work out which one it is?

Answer see page **254**

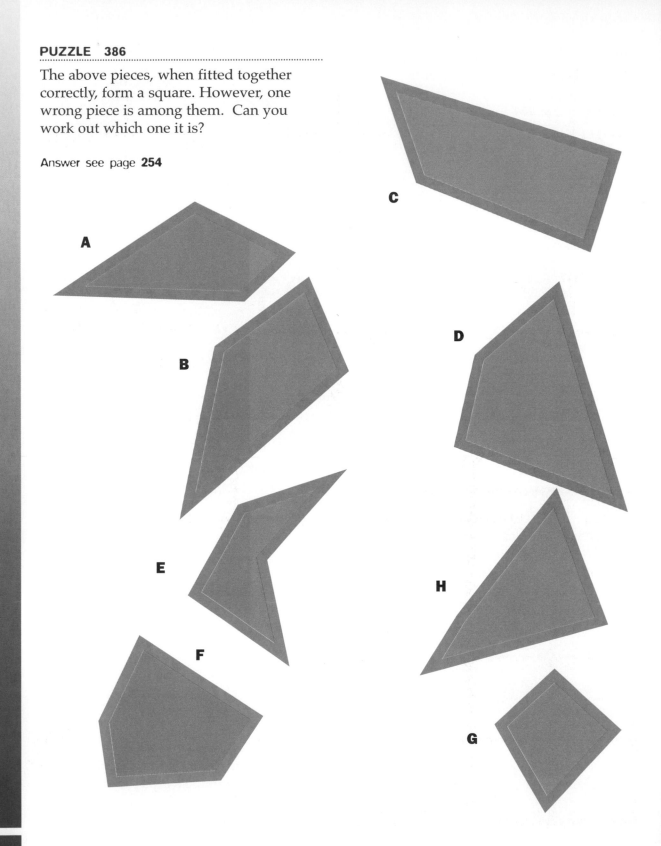

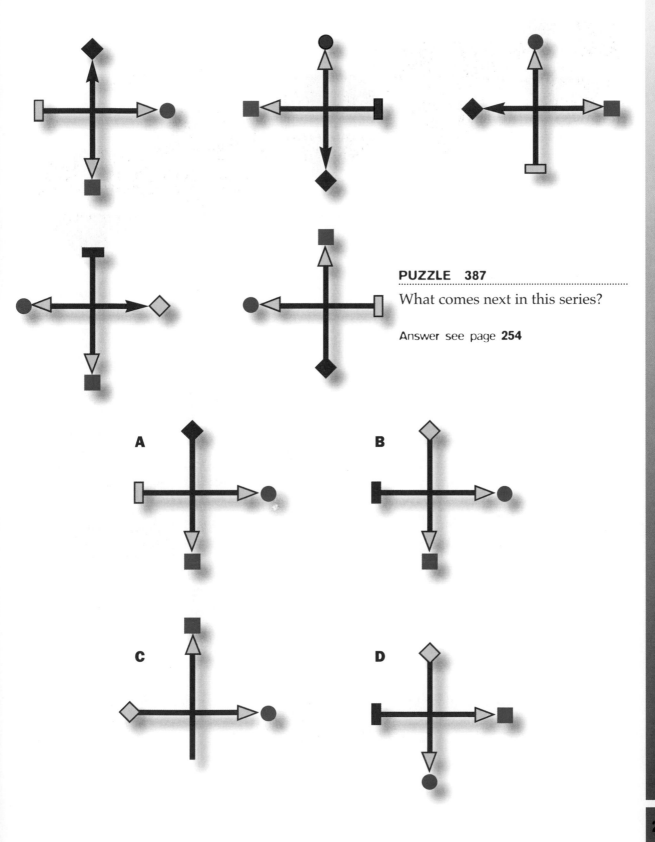

PUZZLE 387

What comes next in this series?

Answer see page **254**

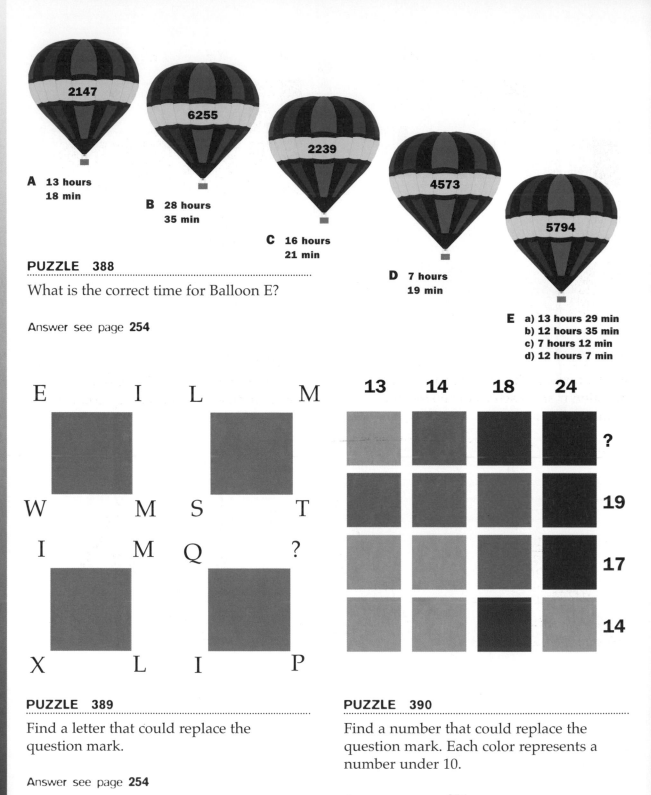

A 13 hours 18 min

B 28 hours 35 min

C 16 hours 21 min

D 7 hours 19 min

E a) 13 hours 29 min
   b) 12 hours 35 min
   c) 7 hours 12 min
   d) 12 hours 7 min

PUZZLE 388

What is the correct time for Balloon E?

Answer see page **254**

PUZZLE 389

Find a letter that could replace the question mark.

Answer see page **254**

PUZZLE 390

Find a number that could replace the question mark. Each color represents a number under 10.

Answer see page **254**

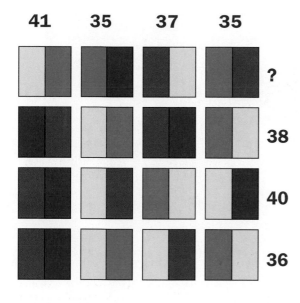

PUZZLE 391

Find a number that could replace the question mark. Each color represents a number under 10

Answer see page **254**

PUZZLE 392

Find a number that could replace the question mark. Each color represents a number under 10.

Answer see page **254**

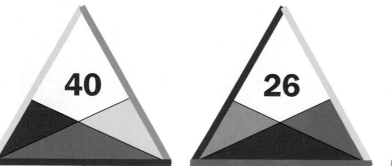

PUZZLE 393

Find a number that could replace the question mark. Each color represents a number under 10.

Answer see page **254**

4	8	3	2	7	5	6	1	9	4	**?**
2	3	7	6	2	4	1	5	3	7	**90**
8	7	3	2	4	6	9	1	4	2	**101**
4	3	6	8	2	9	7	6	8	7	**115**
3	2	1	6	9	8	8	7	3	4	**101**
6	2	3	8	4	1	9	7	2	6	**104**
7	3	4	2	1	9	4	5	3	5	**100**
6	5	4	3	2	8	4	7	6	1	**103**
3	5	2	1	8	6	9	4	3	7	**106**
6	8	7	3	2	4	5	9	5	6	**109**

103 98 99 100 81 117 121 109 99 107

PUZZLE 394

Find a number that could replace the question mark. Each color represents a number under 10. Some may be minus numbers.

Answer see page **255**

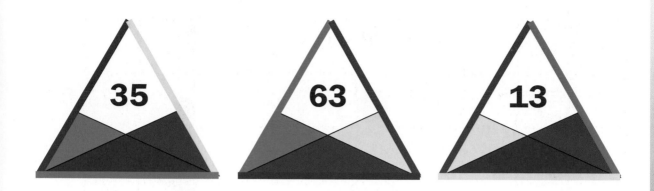

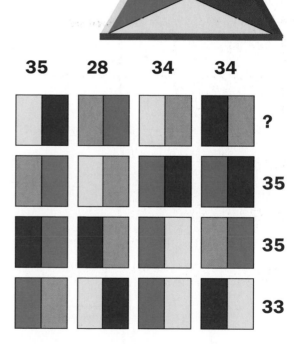

PUZZLE 395

Find a number that could replace the
question mark. Each color represents a
number under 10.

Answer see page **255**

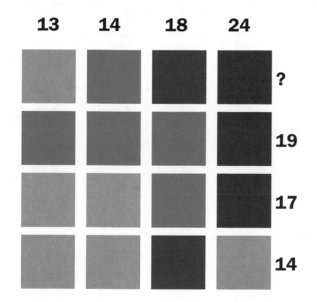

13	14	18	24	
				?
				19
				17
				14

35	28	34	34	
				?
				35
				35
				33

PUZZLE 396

Find a number that could replace the
question mark. Each color represents a
number under 10

Answer see page **255**

PUZZLE 397

Find a number that could replace the
question mark. Each color represents a
number under 10.

Answer see page **255**

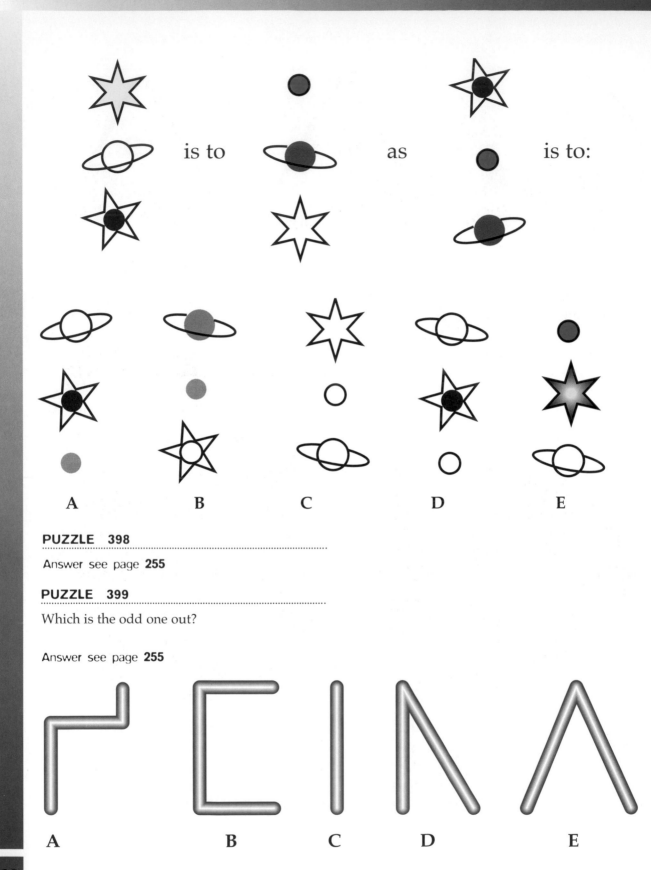

PUZZLE 398

Answer see page **255**

PUZZLE 399

Which is the odd one out?

Answer see page **255**

A   B   C   D   E

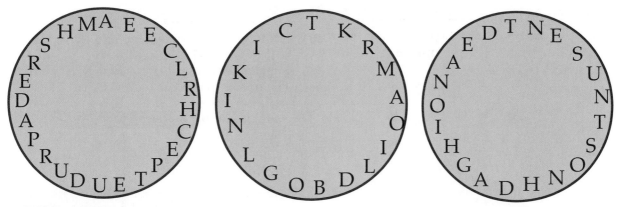

PUZZLE 400

The circles of letters above contain the names of three works of literature (one French, one from the Middle East, one American). Can you unravel them?

Answer see page **255**

PUZZLE 401

Have a look at the strange watches below. By cracking the logic that connects them you should be able to work out what time should be shown on the face of the fifth watch.

Answer see page **255**

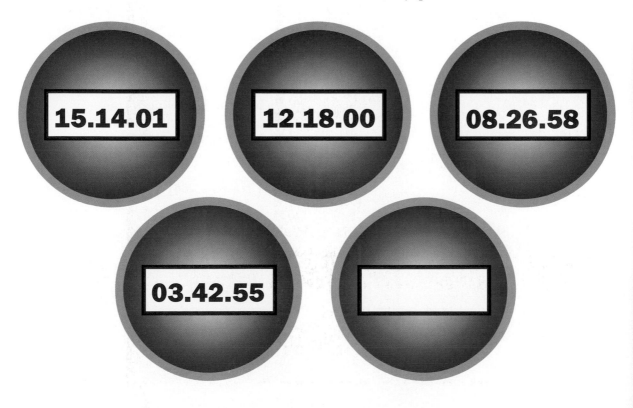

PUZZLE 402

Take 9 matches or toothpicks and lay them out in 3 triangles. By moving 3 matches try to make 5 triangles.

Answer see page 255

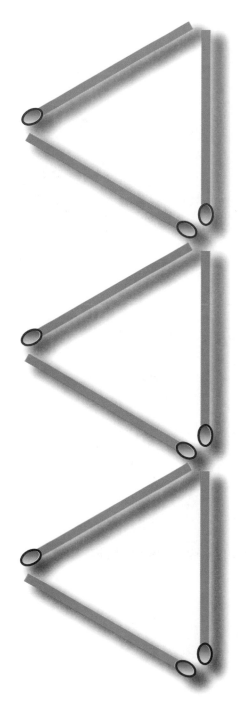

PUZZLE 403

If you look at the grid carefully you will be able to find the names of three international airports cunningly concealed. The names wind through the grid like a snake so, once you have discovered one of them, it should be possible to discover the others.

Answer see page 255

A	L	M	A	S
P	I	O	N	G
S	R	B	E	A
A	U	G	N	T
L	K	C	I	W

PUZZLE 404

Which of the following forms a perfect circle when combined with the diagram on the right?

Answer see page 255

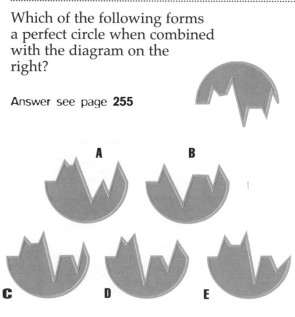

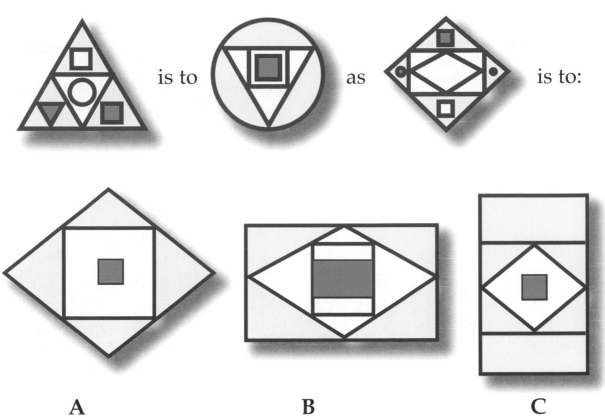

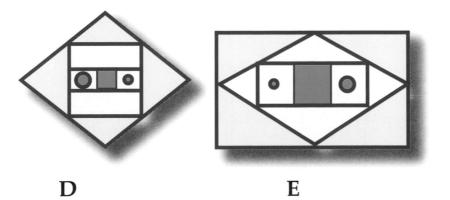

A   B   C

D   E

PUZZLE   405

Answer see page **255**

PUZZLE 406

Which cube can be made using:

Answer see page **255**

A   B   C   D   E

PUZZLE 407

Which is the odd one out?

Answer see page **255**

A   B   C   D   E

PUZZLE 408

What comes next in the sequence?

Answer see page **255**

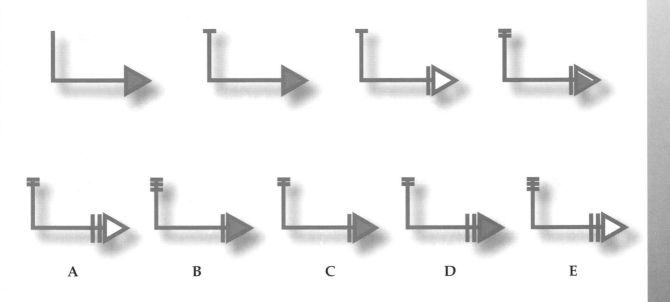

A   B   C   D   E

PUZZLE 409

Try to work out the fiendish logic behind
this series of clocks and replace the
question mark.

Answer see page **256**

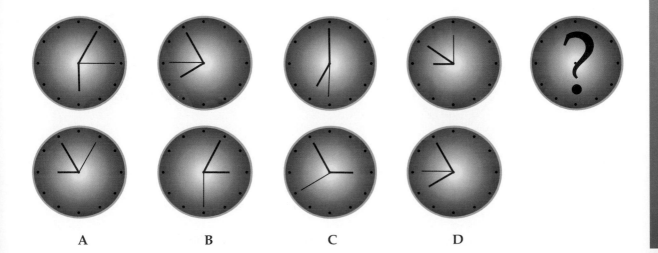

A   B   C   D

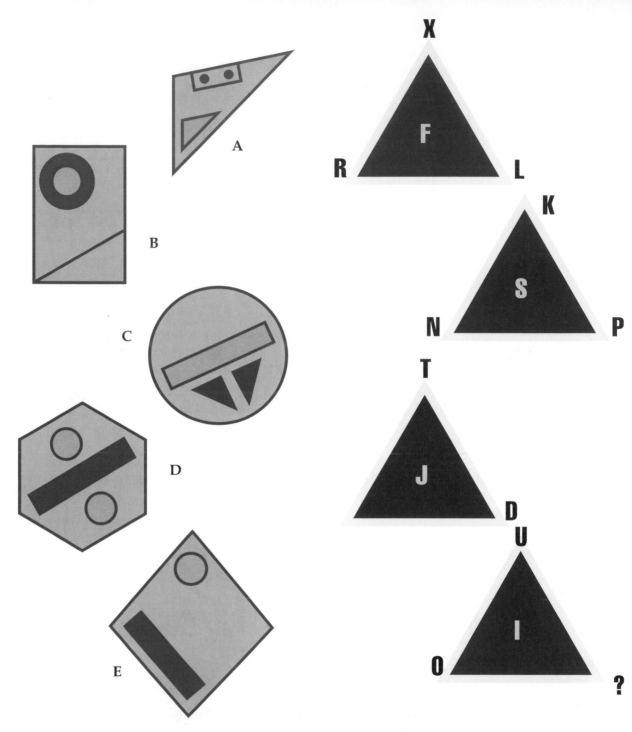

PUZZLE 410

Which is the odd one out?

Answer see page **256**

PUZZLE 411

Look at these triangles. Can you work out what the missing letter is?

Answer see page **256**

238

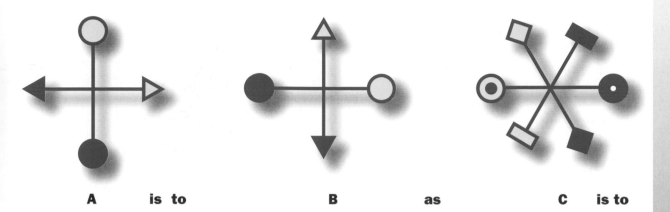

A   is to   B   as   C   is to

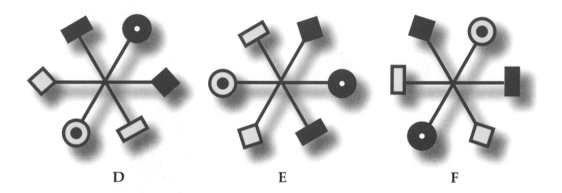

D   E   F

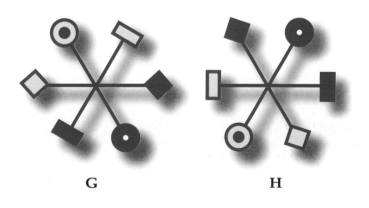

G   H

PUZZLE   412

Answer see page **256**

PUZZLE 413

Which of the following can be constructed using the map to the right:

Answer see page **256**

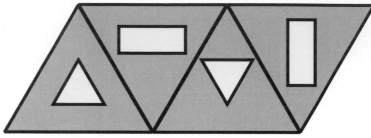

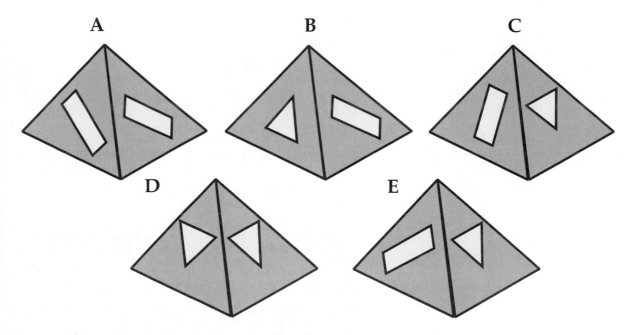

PUZZLE 414

Which is the odd one out?

Answer see page **256**

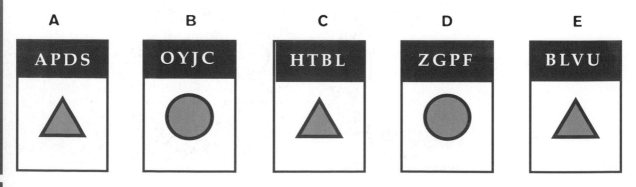

D	A	L	A	M	A	N	D	A	R
E	H	M	A	A	L	A	S	S	E
R	O	N	E	B	I	T	T	E	N
A	C	A	R	K	Z	E	R	A	U
H	H	E	B	E	N	I	T	O	J
O	I	L	L	U	A	G	E	D	S
Y	M	S	O	C	H	A	R	L	E
O	I	A	P	L	E	N	O	T	S
C	N	H	C	I	T	Y	H	O	U
C	M	W	O	R	H	T	A	E	H

PUZZLE 415

Hidden in this grid are 11 international airports. The names follow each other and meander in a snake-like route through the grid. When you discover the first name you should be able to find the other 10.

Answer see page **256**

241

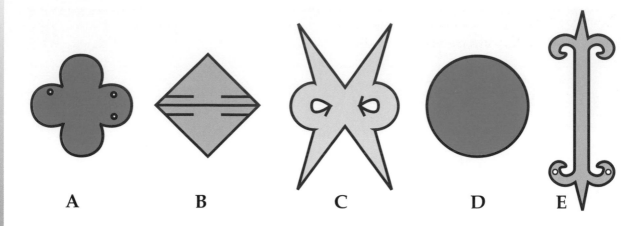

PUZZLE 416

Which is the odd one out?

Answer see page **256**

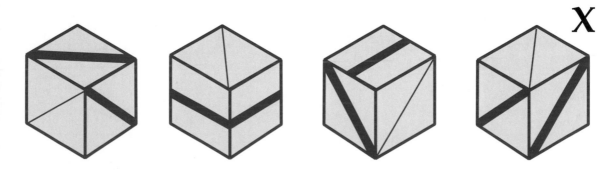

PUZZLE 417

The pictures illustrate different views of one cube. What does the hidden side indicated by the X look like?

Answer see page **256**

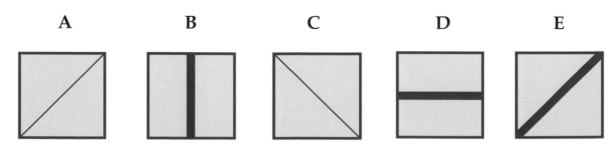

PUZZLE 418

Which of the following comes next in the sequence?

Answer see page **256**

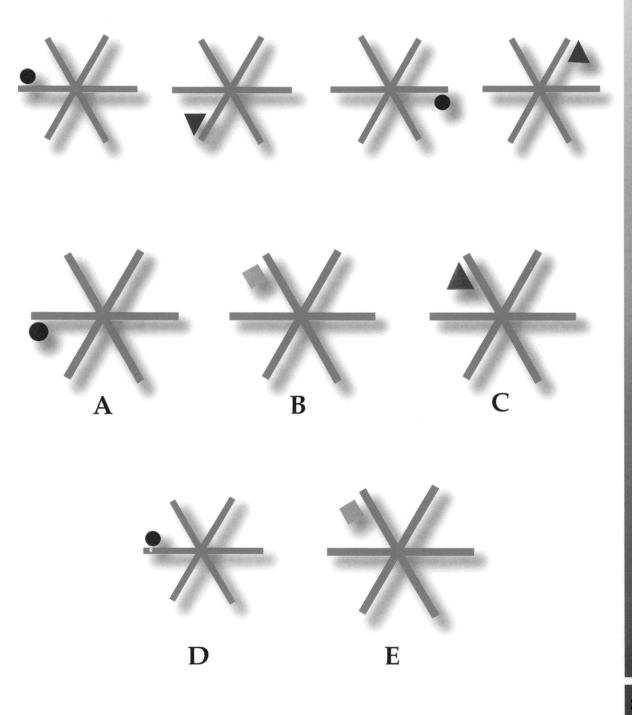

A

B

C

D

E

PUZZLE 419

The values of the segments are 3 consecutive numbers under 10. The yellow is worth 7 and the sum of the segments equals 50. What do the blue and green segments equal?

Answer see page **256**

PUZZLE 420

How much is the question mark worth?

Answer see page **256**

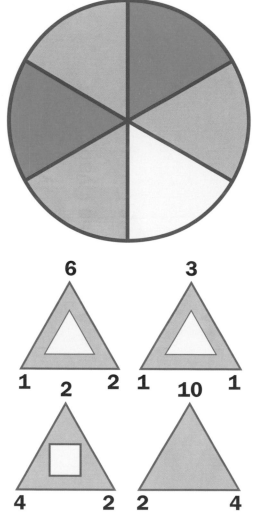

PUZZLE 421

Look at the triangles above. What geometrical shape should logically be placed in the fourth triangle?

Answer see page **256**

PUZZLE 422

Where should another dot belong?

Answer see page **256**

PUZZLE 423

Which comes next in the sequence?

Answer see page **256**

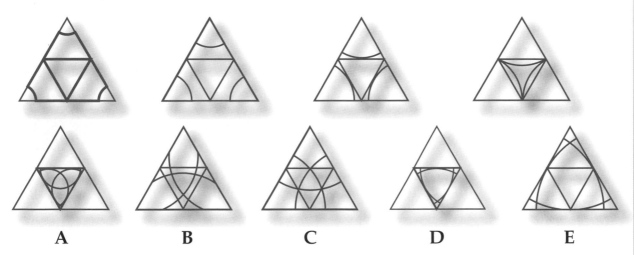

A B C D E

PUZZLE 424

Which is the odd one out?

Answer see page **256**

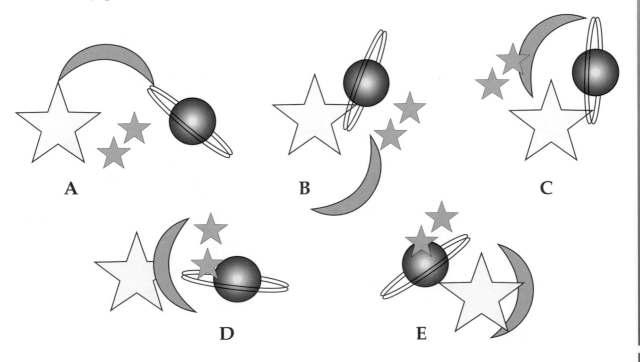

A B C

D E

PUZZLE 425

What comes next in the sequence?

Answer see page **256**

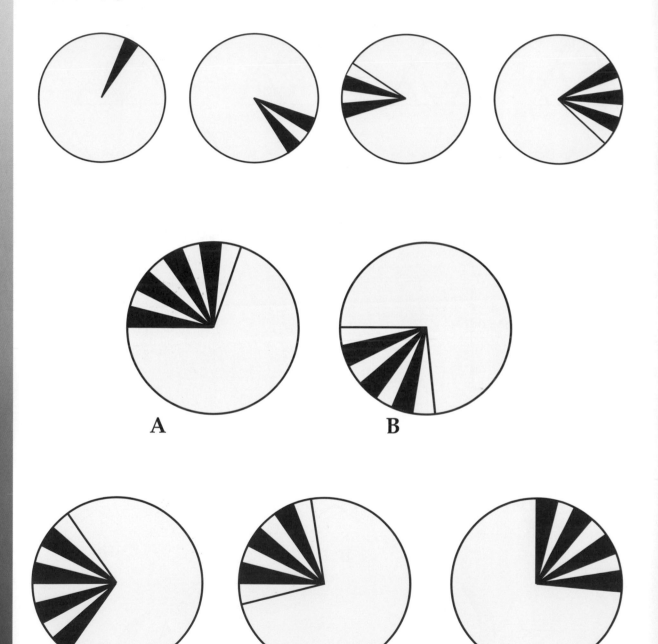

A

B

C

D

E

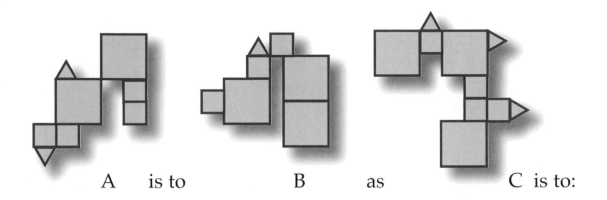

A   is to   B   as   C is to:

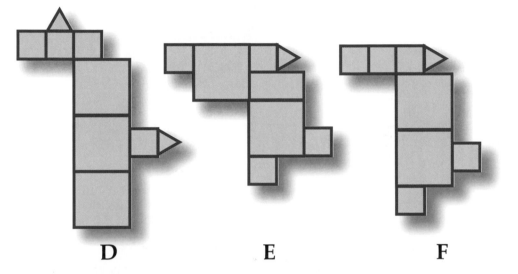

D   E   F

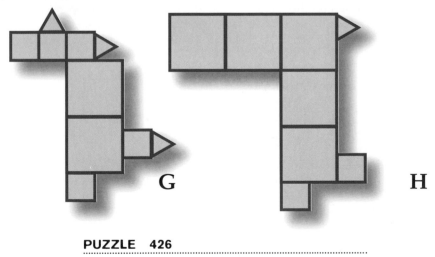

G   H

PUZZLE 426

Answer see page **256**

Answer 286
Costner, Cushing, Dunaway, Garland, Hepburn. The extra one is Domingo.

Answer 287
D. The striped section moves clockwise by 1, 2, 3 and 4 sections (repeat). Each time it moves by 2 and 4 sections the pattern is reflected. The dot moves 2 sections clockwise and 1 section counterclockwise alternately.

Answer 288
The pattern sequence is shown below. Starting at the bottom right, work in a diagonal boustrophedon (clockwise start).

Answer 289
A and N. The series is B, D, F, H, J (2, 4, 6, 8, 10). Add 1, 2, 3, 4, 5, respectively, to the values to get the letters in the second triangle.

Answer 290
19. Write the alphabet in a circle. The numbers represent values of letters based on the alphabet backwards (A = 26, Z = 1). Start at A, miss 2, D (=23), miss 2, G, etc.

Answer 291
Rossini, Puccini, Debussy, Berlioz, Corelli. The extra one is Cezanne.

Answer 292

The starting point is at Row 1, Column 1. The number is 31. Start at the finishing point and work back.

Answer 293

 Start at the top right and move across the square in a horizontal boustrophedon. The pattern is: miss 1 square, turn by 180°, turn by 90° clockwise, miss 1, turn by 90° clockwise, turn by 180°.

Answer 294
Reading across segments 1 and 1a, 2 and 2a, etc., the dots move around the circle in a vertical boustrophedon.

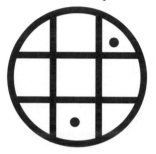

Answer 295
A la Recherche du Temps Perdu by Marcel Proust.

Answer 296
7. Add the three numbers on the outside of each square (A). Add the digits of the sum (B). Divide A by B and place in the small square.

Answer 297
72. Halve the number on the top left, multiply the number on the top right by 3. Multiply the two resulting numbers with each other, and put the product in the bottom square.

Answer 298
C. It is the only circle with an asymmetrical shape.

Answer 299

Answer 300
K. K is the same number of spaces in the alphabet from H and N, O and G, and E and Q.

Answer 301
8. The two numbers added together give the number the minute hand points to on the next clock. The hour hand points to the number three spaces before.

Answer 302
D. Take the values of the first two letters of each starting town, the first based on the alphabet forward (A = 1, Z = 26) and the second on the alphabet backward (A = 26, Z = 1). Add the values together. The new letter of that value will be the first letter of the new town.

Answer 303
Brezhnev, Disraeli, Thatcher, Adenauer, Pompidou.

Answer 304
S. D is the 4th letter from the start of the alphabet, W is the 4th from the end. F is the 6th from the start, U the 6th from the end, etc.

Answer 305
38. Regard the alphabet as a circle. The number is double the number of spaces between the letters.

Answer 306
11. Divide the number of sides of the letter by 2 and add the value of the letter, based on its position in the alphabet.

Answer 307

		2
9		7
4	8	3

Answer 308
The pattern sequence is shown below. It starts at the top right and works down in a diagonal boustrophedon (counterclockwise start).

Answer 309
D. These are the first letters of Do, Re, Mi, Fa, So, La, Tee, etc.

Answer 310
M. Add 9 to the value of each letter in the first circle. C + 9 = L.

Answer 311
N. The letters spell Wittgenstein.

Answer 312
B.

HARD ANSWERS HARD ANSWERS HARD ANSWERS HARD ANSWERS HARD ANSWERS HARD

Answer 313

The pattern is:

Answer 314

10. Multiply the two numbers on the outside of each segment, divide the product by 1,2,3 …8 respectively and put the new number in the middle of the opposite segment.

Answer 315

Hockney, Matisse, Gauguin, Hogarth, Vermeer. The extra one is Erasmus.

Answer 316

C. All the others, when reflected on a vertical line, have an identical partner.

Answer 317

M. The value of the letter on the bottom left, based on its alphabetical position, minus the value of the letter on the bottom right, results in the letter in the middle. Incidentally, the outer letters spell Mark Twain backwards, but this is of no significance.

Answer 318

C. The letters spell Henry Mancini backwards.

Answer 319

32. All the others have a partner, with the digits being reversed.

Answer 320

The extra word is Arrivederci.

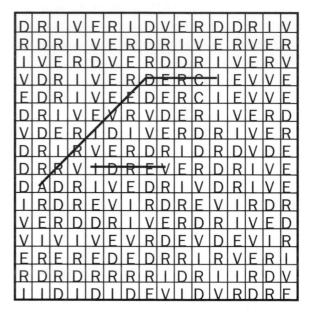

Answer 321

C. A and D, and B and E are pairs. When reflected against a vertical line and turned, they are identical.

Answer 322

W. Starting from P go back 3 spaces in alphabet (M), forward 3 (S), back 5 (K), forward 5 (U), back 7 (I), forward 7.

Answer 323

U. The letters spell Art Garfunkel.

Answer 324

Belmondo, Pfeiffer, Rampling, Redgrave, Travolta.

Answer 325

D and E.

Answer 326

O and V. The others spell Charlie Chaplin.

Answer 327

The pattern starts at the top right and goes in diagonal stripes from left to right.

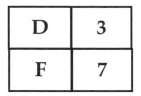

D	3
F	7

Answer 328

56. Take 2/3 of the number in the top left square and multiply it by twice the number in the top right square. Put the new number in the bottom square.

Answer 329

I. These are the second letters of the numbers one to five.

Answer 330

9. The alphabet equivalents make up the name Nagasaki.

Answer 331

There are 43 pairs.

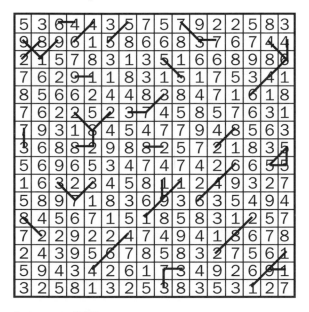

Answer 332

Anouilh, Moliere, Ionesco, Osborne, Marlowe. The extra name is Connery.

Answer 333

5. Add both numbers in one segment, add the digits of that sum and place new number in the next segment, going clockwise.

Answer 334

22. Regard the alphabet as a circle. The number equates to the spaces between letters.

Answer 335

8. Starting at the top left corner add the first three numbers and place the sum on the inside of the second number. Moving around the square in a clockwise spiral, repeat with the next three numbers, etc.

Answer 336

C. Add together the values of the letters (Z = 1, A = 26) and subtract the individual digits from the sum.

Answer 337

B. Each column contains faces with 4 different types of hair, pairs of ears, eyes, mouths and face shapes.

Answer 338

54. The colors are worth Pink 3, Orange 4, Yellow 5, Green 6, Purple -2, Red -4.

Answer 339

141. The colors are worth Red 2, Green 4, Orange 7, Yellow 9. Multiply the numbers in each square together.

Answer 340

17. The colors are worth Red 6, Yellow 7, Green 10, Orange 12. In each square subtract the lower color from the upper. The colors represent numbers but are NOT necessarily under 10.

Answer 341

57, 71, 53, 45. The colors are worth Blue 3, Yellow 5, Orange -4, Green -5. Multiply the two top numbers in each square and add them to the product of the two bottom numbers. Then add or subtract according to the color of the square.

HARD ANSWERS HARD ANSWERS HARD ANSWERS HARD ANSWERS HARD ANSWERS

Answer 342
96. The colors are worth Pink 2, Yellow 3, Green 4, Orange 5.

Answer 343
90. Colors are worth Orange 25, Purple 17, Yellow 36, Green 12.

Answer 344
Yellow. The colors are in alphabetical order: Blue, Green, Mauve, Orange, Purple, Red, White.

Answer 345

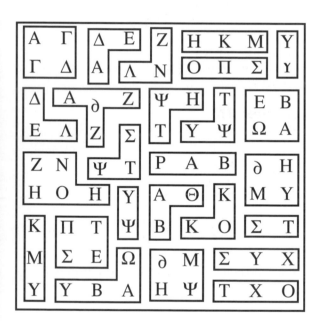

Answer 346
The minute hand should be on the 4, the hour hand on the 8. The numbers the hands are pointing to are doubles of each other. The lower number moves forward by 1 each time, with the hands being reversed.

Answer 347
T. E is the 5th letter from the start of the alphabet, V is the 5th from the end. D is the 4th from the beginning, W is the 4th from the end, etc.

Answer 348
Z. Add the values of the three outside numbers, based on their position in the alphabet, and place their sum in the inner box opposite.

Answer 349
410. In all the others the first two digits added equal the third.

Answer 350
The pattern sequence is shown below. It starts at the top left and works downwards in a vertical boustrophedon.

Answer 351
V. It spells Anton Chekhov.

Answer 352
S. Add the values of the letters on the top and right, and the values of the letters on the left and bottom. Subtract the second sum from the first, and put either the new number or alternately the letter based on the value of that number into the middle.

Answer 353

The shapes form a series in order of value:

Answer 354
20. Left hand x right hand ÷ waist = head. Left foot x right foot ÷ waist = head.

Answer 355
Start at the top right and move in a counterclockwise spiral. The dot moves clockwise around the square.

Answer 356
C and F.

Answer 357
Z. In alternate shapes go: top, left, middle, right, bottom, and left, top, middle, bottom, right. In both cases miss out one letter.

Answer 358
M. Starting with the middle triangle and letter A move round the diagram in a clockwise direction. Move then on to the diagram on the right and last to the diagram on the left. Miss three letters with each move.

Answer 359
A.

Answer 360
A. The edges of all the symbols in one square added together, increase by 2 with each square (i.e. 12, 14, 16, 18, 20)

Answer 361
D. The formula is: left + (middle x right) = top + (middle x bottom), but in D, the answers are 26 and 25 respectively.

Answer 362
R. These are the second letters of the days of the week.

Answer 363
7. Multiply the two numbers on the outside of each segment, divide their product by 2 and place the new number two segments ahead in the middle.

Answer 364
P. Write the alphabet in a circle. NOP are the letters diametrically opposite ABC.

Answer 365
20. Take two numbers in adjacent circles. If both are odd, add them. If both are even, multiply them. If one number is odd and one is even take the difference. Put the new number in the overlapping section.

Answer 366
 The formula is (right x left – top) x black fraction of circle = bottom.

Answer 367
The hidden letter is F. The pattern is diagonal stripes starting from the top right and going up from right to left.

Answer 368
5 and 625. The cubes of 7, 9 and 13 go into the right-hand circle, the squares of 18, 26 and 54 go into the left-hand circle.

Answer 369
F. Each shape changes into a shape with 2 extra sides. The order of shapes is reversed.

Answer 370
B and E.

Answer 371
The pattern sequence is:

Start at top left and follow the pattern in a clockwise spiral.

Answer 372
27 or 729. The numbers are part of a sequence that alternates A^3, B, C^3, D, E^3, ...

Answer 373
11. Multiply the number of sides of each number by 3, and then subtract the number printed.

Answer 374
56. (Head x left foot) ÷ waist = right hand; (head x right foot) ÷ waist = left hand). (14 x 15) ÷ 5 = 42; (14 x 20) ÷ 5 (56).

Answer 375
9. Multiply the two outer numbers in each segment, and divide the product by 2 and 3 alternately. Place the new number in the middle of the opposite segment.

Answer 376
E. The squares with lines from the bottom left to the top right have arrows pointing up or right. Squares with lines from the bottom right to the top left have arrows pointing down or left.

Answer 377
A Midsummer Night's Dream by William Shakespeare.

Answer 378
G.

Answer 379
11. It is a series of prime numbers.

Answer 380
D. The formula is: (right x shaded fraction of left) – (top x shaded fraction of bottom) = middle shape's number of sides. Therefore, in example D: (18 x ⅔ [12]) – (12 x ¾) [9] = 3. The answer shape should be 3-sided, so it is the odd one out.

Answer 381
T. It spells Marcel Proust.

Answer 382
D. The whole figure is reflected on a horizontal line. Any shape with straight lines is then rotated by 90° clockwise and a dot in a round shape disappears.

Answer 383
B and F.

Answer 384
91. All the others are prime numbers.

Answer 385
5. Three numbers in a horizontal line add up to the fourth number.

Answer 386
D.

Answer 387
E. The symbols turn by 180° and 90° alternately. The circle and square swap places, the diamond and rectangle swap shading.

Answer 388
A. Multiply first and last digits> Subtract second digit for hours and third for minutes.

Answer 389
E. The outer letters are displaced four places in the alphabet (Eg, E = A, I = E, etc). The answers have then been swapped in adjacent pairs of squares. aeGis, hiPpo, eiGht, maPle.

Answer 390
19. Colors are worth Orange 3, Green 4, Red 5, Purple 7.

Answer 391
34. The colors are worth Green 3, Red 4, Yellow 5, Purple 7. Add colors in each square together.

Answer 392
26. The colors are worth Red 3, Yellow 6, Purple 8, Green 9.

Answer 393
77. The colors are worth Purple 3, Green 4, Yellow 6, Orange 9. Add the left side to the right side and multiply by the base. This is Result 1. Now add the two upper internal colors and subtract the lower. This is Result 2. Then subtract Result 2 from Result 1.

Answer 394
105. The colors are worth Yellow 4, Pink 5, Green 6, Orange 7. Add the value of the color to the number in each square.

Answer 395
27. The colors are worth Yellow 2, , Red 3, Green 4, Purple 6. Multiply the sides of the triangle together to get Result 1. Add the inner numbers together to get result 2. Now subtract R2 from R1 to get the answer.

Answer 396
19. The colors are worth Orange 3, Red 5, Purple 7, Green 4. Add colors in the same square together.

Answer 397
28. Colors are worth Purple 5, Orange 2, Yellow 3, Green 6. Each color represents a number under 10.

Answer 398
D. An unshaded ringed planet becomes a shaded ringed planet; a star containing a shaded planet becomes an unshaded planet; a shaded ringed planet becomes an unshaded ringed planet; an unshaded planet becomes a star containing a shaded planet. The symbols are then vertically reflected.

Answer 399
A. In the other cases the addition of a vertical or horizontal straight line would form a capital letter.

Answer 400
A la Recherche du Temps Perdu, A Thousand and One Nights, To Kill a Mockingbird.

Answer 401
The hours move back 3, 4, 5, and 6 hours. The minutes move forward 4, 8, 16, and 32 minutes. The seconds move back 1, 2, 3, and 4 seconds. The time on the fifth watch should be 21:14:51.

Answer 402

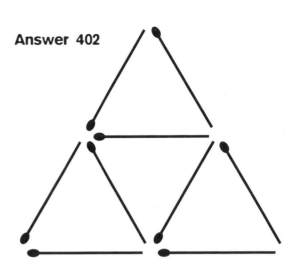

Answer 403
Ben Gurion, Gatwick, Las Palmas.

Answer 404
C.

Answer 405
A. The inner shape becomes outer shape, the shape surrounding it fits inside, then shape at top. The remainder is then shrunk and put inside the middle shape. A shaded shape covers an unshaded shape.

Answer 406
A.

Answer 407
D. In all other cases the number of cross pieces on top of each vertical line is multiplied by the number of cross pieces on the bottom. All give even answers apart from D.

Answer 408
D. Add a cross piece each time, alternating between adding them vertically and horizontally. A vertical cross piece changes the color of the arrow head.

Answer 409
D. The second hand moves forward 30 and back 15 seconds alternately, the minute hand moves back 10 and forward 5 minutes alternately, and the hour hand moves forward 2 hours and back 1 hour alternately.

Answer 410
D.

Answer 411
O. The letters represent a number based on their position in the alphabet. The total for each triangle equals 60.

Answer 412
E. Rotate one place clockwise and then reflect across a horizontal line through the middle of the figure.

Answer 413
A.

Answer 414
E. The value of letter given by position in the alphabet is added together. An even answer should give a triangle, an odd answer a circle.

Answer 415
Heathrow, McCoy, O'Hare, Dalaman, Dar Es Salaam, Ho Chi Minh City, Houston, El Paso, Charles De Gaulle, Benito Juarez, Kranebitten.

Answer 416
E. Left half reflected to form symmetrical shape, then half of right half is reflected back.

Answer 417
D.

Answer 418
D. Circle and triangle alternate. After a circle the next figure moves around 1 space, staying on the same side of the line. After a triangle it moves on 2.

Answer 419
Blue = 8; Green = 9.

Answer 420
1. Starting with 64, subtract 1, 2, 4, 8, 16, 32, missing a number each time and working in a clockwise direction.

Answer 421
A square. If the three numbers around the triangle add to an even number the shape is a square; if it is odd, then it is another triangle.

Answer 422
Penultimate triangle on the bottom row. Sequence, starting from the top and working from left to right, of dot, miss 1 triangle, dot, miss 2, dot, miss 3, dot, miss 4.

Answer 423
C. Curved lines gradually encroach on space within triangle.

Answer 424
D. One tip of the star is missing.

Answer 425
C.

Answer 426
C. Small square becomes a big square and vice versa. A small square with a triangle goes to small square alone. A triangle on big square remains a triangle.